Hear Me Now

Tragedy in Cambodia

Hear Me Now

Tragedy in Cambodia

By
Sophal Leng Stagg
As Told To
W. E. Stagg and Jack Sandler, Ph.D.

MANCORP PUBLISHING, INC.
Tampa, Florida

Typesetting by JA Studios
Cover design by The Mesa Group

Library of Congress Cataloging-in-Publication Data
Stagg, Sophal Leng, 1965 –

      Hear me now: tragedy in Cambodia/by Sophal Leng Stagg as told to W. E. Stagg and Jack Sandler.

      p. cm.

      ISBN 0-931541-66-2

      1. Cambodia -- Politics and government -- 1975- 2. Political atrocities -- Cambodia. 3. Stagg, Sophal Leng, 1965-. I. Stagg, W. E. (William E.), 1950- . II. Sandler, Jack, 1929- . III. Title
DS554.8.S7 1997
959.604'2'092--dc21   97-11110
[B]   CIP

Manufactured in the United States of America

ISBN 0-931541-66-2

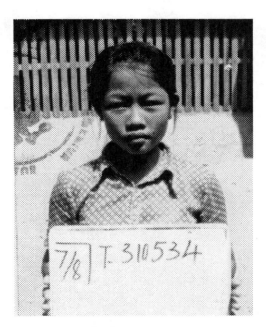

Sophal Leng, 1980

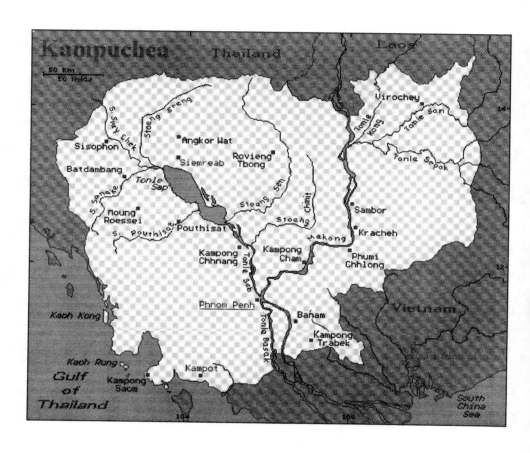

Preface

In April of 1975, after many years of turmoil, the civil struggle between several political factions in Cambodia culminated in the capture of the capital city of Phnom Penh by the Marxist Khmer Rouge regime. Under the leadership of a terrorist with the unlikely name of Pol Pot, the new regime callously imposed a Maoist style revolution on the Cambodian people. During the four years in which they remained in power, about two million Cambodians died as the result of starvation, torture and execution. An even greater number were displaced and an ancient and revered civilization was virtually extinguished. This holocaust, while well documented in such treatments as the movie "The Killing Fields" and in the autobiography by Haing Ngor has been almost totally ignored outside of Southeast Asia. If, however, we have learned nothing in the continuing struggle of man's inhumanity to man, we can confidently state that such "lessons" in history will be repeated as long as they are overlooked by the world community. The continuing reliance upon witnesses to such events serves as a constant reminder of the need to bring them to our attention.

One such witness is Sophal Leng Stagg, who was nine years old when she and her family were forced to leave their home in Phnom Penh in April of 1975, joining the millions of Cambodians whose lives were devastated by the Khmer Rouge. It is with the purpose of serving as a witness that she has related the details of her experiences during the four years that she and her family lived under the oppression imposed by this brutal regime.

SECURITY REGULATIONS*

1.   You must answer accordingly to my questions. Do not turn them away.

2.   Do not try to hide the facts by making pretexts of this and that. You are strictly prohibited to contest me.

3.   Do not be a fool for you are a person who dared to thwart the revolution.

4.   You must immediately answer my questions without wasting time to reflect.

5.   Do not tell me about your immoralities or the essence of the revolution.

6.   While getting lashes or electrification you must <u>NOT</u> cry out at all.

7.   Do nothing; sit still and wait for my orders. When I ask you to do something you must do it without protesting.

8. Do not make pretexts about Kampuchea in order to hide your traitorous jaw.

9. If you do not follow the above rules you will receive many lashes of electric wire.

10. If you disobey any point of my regulations you will either get ten lashes or five electric discharges.

These ten regulations are an English translation of a sign at *Tuol Sleng* prison in which over sixteen thousand political prisoners were executed by the Khmer Rouge. It now serves as a museum documenting one phase of the atrocities committed by the followers of Pol Pot.

(*Reprinted from an article originally published in the *National Geographic*, May, 1982.)

The courage of her family during their captivity, together with Sophal's "dream" is truly inspirational. Sophal's burning desire to see a peaceful non-violent world continues to this day. The intense respect for others that exists within Sophal complements her strong will to live in a gentle and caring world. Sophal wishes to be heard so that her experiences will hopefully have a positive impact on our world as we know it today.

SOPHAL'S DREAM

My world, sometimes harsh and cruel
  Will my life end this day?

Sometimes kind and gentle
  Sometimes changing by the day

Which way will it end
  Dream on, dream on, wait another day

I have the pain as so many do
  Dream on, dream on, wait another day

My dreams are there but not known where
  Find them and live another day

My cries not heard, not heard this day
  No, I will not die this way

Stop the pain for now, and then
  Let me live in peace one more day

My world is hurt as am I
  The joy long gone - must I say goodbye?

Not today; it's not my time
  Dream on, dream on, wait another day

1

Twenty years and what seems like a dozen lifetimes have passed since the events that I describe in the following pages transpired and, although I can now look back with less emotion, the memories of that time are as vivid as if they happened yesterday. I cannot completely explain my reasons for the need to write about these experiences except as a testimony to those whose lives were lost and who can no longer speak for themselves.

I was nine years old in April of 1975 and living with my family in Phnom Penh. There were six children living with my father, Kim, and my mother Na, in our home. My oldest brother, Choeun, had married Kim Run and moved to Battdambang four years earlier where he owned a pharmacy. My second oldest brother, Thom, together with his wife, Savvy, and her parents lived in another part of the capital city. My other siblings, 23-year old Thouch, 21-year old Chantha, 19-year old Than, 13-year old Thoeun, and my 10-year old sister, Chan, were still living with our parents according to Cambodian tradition. My father, whom I called Papa, was 52 years old and an official in the Lon Nol government. We were practicing Buddhists, the primary religion of Cambodia, and all of us had been or were being educated in the public school system. My

48-year old mother, who we called Ma was the vitality that held the pieces together, as was true of the family system in general in my country.

The city was in a festive mood in anticipation of the three-day Cambodian New Year, the most important holiday of the year. Despite the continuing conflict in the countryside between the opposing military factions, the city was decorated with bright colored banners, and every house was topped with a new angel, referred to in our language as "*theravada*." Over the next three days, in addition to gift-giving, each family would rededicate itself to the belief that one's life is personally enhanced through kindness to and respect for others. Most families would share their food and possessions with the monks in the temples. In the midst of our preparations, a letter arrived from Choeun asking my mother to join him to help him with his wife, who was close to giving birth to their second child. Up to then, we had not been seriously affected by the conflict between the Lon Nol regime and the Maoist Khmer Rouge, but, for some reason, the prospect of my mother leaving us at this time left me terribly unhappy and perhaps, in a child's mind, was related to the growing uneasiness among the citizens that our lives were going to change for the worse. We knew little of the actual struggle between the various forces, but almost daily, we could hear the rumbling of bombs exploding on the outskirts of the city. I wanted to be reassured that our lives were not threatened, and any change in our plans to celebrate the New Year would have been devastating. Imagine my joy when she told us that she had decided my brother, Thouch, would be going to Battdambang and that she would remain with us to continue our celebration.

Over the next several days, my parents attempted to maintain our customary preparations even though the news from the countryside kept getting worse. We could detect the concern in their voices when they discussed the flight of many of Cambodia's politicians and wealthy families in the face of a possible takeover by the Khmer Rouge. The day before the New Year a sense of hysteria descended on the city. People were in the streets running in different directions; children were crying and our parents were finding it increasingly difficult to maintain a normal routine. When my mother heard that the airport had closed the day after Thouch left for Battdambang, she was near panic, since this meant that my third brother would not be able to return from his visit with my brother. That night we prayed for his safety. Our family was deeply religious and prayer offered peace and hope. We would soon discover that such practices would be forbidden by the new regime.

On the night of April 16, 1975, we were awakened by the terrible sound of bombs and guns, close at hand. The explosions were so near that our house shook with each burst. To the mind of a terrified nine-year old girl, it seemed that the gunfire was aimed directly at me. My parents led us to a shelter underneath the house and there, in total darkness, my mother clutched my sister, Chan, and me to her body and comforted us with her warmth and love. Although she must have been as frightened as we were, her first thought was for the safety of her children. Needless to say, none of us slept that night.

Early the next morning, Papa went out to inquire about the circumstances of the battle. We huddled together in one room hoping for the best, but fearing the worst. When he returned, we could tell from the worried expression on his face and the change in his demeanor that the news was foreboding. He told us that the Khmer Rouge were everywhere, marching up and down the highways waving their flags and celebrating their victory at the conquest of the capital city. Although he was clearly concerned for our welfare, my own reaction was to hope that this new development would at least put an end to the warfare and the killing. Maybe now, I thought, Cambodia would once again be at peace and my family could return to our treasured customs. I soon learned that this was a false hope and that the people I loved the most would begin to experience the worst horrors imaginable.

Later that day we found out that the entire capital had stopped functioning—stores, schools, and government offices were closed and every street was blocked with barricades ending any attempt to travel. In the place of the usual sights and sounds that I had grown to associate with the city that had been my home all of my life were the Khmer Rouge. Their presence was everywhere, particularly shocking and ominous because of their stark black uniforms and the weapons that they carried with them. I remember noticing that their sandals were made out of old tires which was completely out of character with Cambodian custom. It was as if the city had been transformed in an instant, like a friendly welcoming neighbor who greets you with open arms one second and then changes into an ugly menacing creature in an eye blink. The expression on the faces of our friends conveyed the uncertainty which now faced us. This reaction was soon replaced with the stark realization of what our future portended. The fear was just beginning.

At 12:30 that afternoon, we were jolted by the sound of loud knocking at the front door. Papa opened it and he was confronted by five members of the Khmer Rouge with hostile, menacing expressions. They ordered us to prepare to leave the house as soon as possible for, as they said, our own protection in case the fighting resumed. This, of course, was simply a trick.

We started packing immediately, but the Khmer Rouge continued to harass us with warnings and threats while we rushed to get our possessions together. We didn't know what to take, where we would be going, how long we would be gone—simple questions which anyone would ask under such circumstances were met with gun pointing and threats that we would be killed if we resisted. I now knew how a person feels who is told to do something under threat of harm and is then threatened for not complying fast enough. We were close to a state of paralysis. We ended by taking only as much clothing and food as we were able to carry. Everything else we were forced to leave behind.

Finally, just as we were about to depart, my second oldest brother, Thom, and his wife, Savvy, and her family, arrived to join us. They had been similarly forced to depart by the Khmer Rouge and, at least, we could take some small comfort in that we would be traveling together wherever we should be directed.

I remember the last moments when we left our house with remarkable clarity, despite the fact that 20 years has passed. I have since read of people whose lives had changed dramatically in an instant as the result of some catastrophe and were able to recall the experience in every detail and so it is with me. As we walked into the street we stopped to look at the house that had been the center of all of my experiences for so long. My parents had lived there for over 30 years when they first married. My mother had seen her family change and grow from when she and Papa were newly-wed and faced the future with courage and love. Eight children were born to them while they had lived in that home. They had instilled the virtues of our religion in each of us: a love of family, of learning, a sense of community and a commitment to each new generation. Even though my oldest brother, Choeun, had married and he and his wife, Kim Run, lived in Battdambang, and my second oldest brother, Thom, had married Savvy, we maintained close ties with them and often celebrated important occasions together. Surely my mother was overwhelmed by the flood of these memories as we turned to take one last look at our home. Perhaps she knew in some way we would never return and our lives would be changed forever.

What began as a hasty departure from our home and neighborhood soon became a massed confluence of families in an ever-growing crush of frightened, confused humanity. The Khmer Rouge had restricted travel from the city to a handful of streets which soon became crowded with thousands of departing people who, with every step, were transformed from ordinary, orderly citizens into a mad crush of bewildered refugees with children screaming for their parents who were, in turn, wide-eyed with panic, having been separated from their children. My mother urged us to clutch one another's hands as tightly as possible out of fear of also being separated. In this fashion, tight little bands of families were pushed and prodded by the Khmer Rouge with their ear-shattering bull horns, constantly screaming insults while forcing everyone to move faster than was possible, their faces fixed in a permanent expression of hatred.

Soon, for the first time, but what was certainly not to be the last, we came upon the bodies of men, women and children lying dead by the side of the road. The first sight of these experiences strikes against you like a shock wave, and we all shrank with horror at the scene. Later, after constant exposure to such horrors, we soon learned to control our emotions, but the impact of seeing bodies in the open never left us. As the afternoon wore on, the streets became so crowded that our pace slowed to about 50 yards per hour. This, in turn, increased the wrath of the Khmer Rouge who were now screaming at the crowds and firing their weapons in the air, as if we were cattle being herded to the slaughter. By mid-afternoon, the heat was intense and suffocating. The smoke from the burning city added to the nightmare and hundreds of people fell from exhaustion to lie on the side of the road. Before long, the Khmer Rouge were firing their guns at those unfortunates who simply were unable to maintain the rapid pace. These actions created even greater panic among the crowd.

By sunset, and now thoroughly exhausted, many of us still had not completely evacuated the city. We had been walking since about noon with no sense of direction. Nevertheless, there was no respite from the Khmer Rouge who continued to prod us on. As the sun set behind us, we turned to look back at the city that we had come to love with its beautiful lights and buildings. The darkening sky was now red with the fierce glow of a thousand fires. It seemed to us that the whole city was in flames. As the evening progressed, the wind sharpened and we watched in silence as the flames raced on, engulfing trees, homes, offices, destroying everything in its wake. Now, perhaps for the first time, I knew that my house was gone, and with this realization came the crushing fact that Cambodia would never be the same and that this new regime was dedicated to eradicating any hope that things might some day revert back to normal.

At about 9 o'clock that night, a new sense of apprehension spread through the crowd. We soon discovered the cause—we were approaching a gas storage facility and, with the wind driving the fire ever closer at hand, we knew there was a strong possibility of an explosion. The level of panic increased among the refugees surging to avoid the gas tanks. Fortunately, as we were herded closer to the area, the wind suddenly shifted and we half-ran half-walked until we were out of danger.

It was very late that night before we were allowed to stop. We lay where we dropped in the street, too exhausted and frightened to seek any degree of comfort. I fell asleep that night with the curb as my pillow. Had it been only last night since I was asleep in my own bed with a real pillow? The morning came all too soon and Papa started us on our unplanned journey almost as soon as we were up, in order to avoid the crush of the people. By 9 o'clock, however, the streets were as crowded as the day before with everyone pushing and shoving, parents still searching for lost children, children crying hysterically out of fear or hunger or having been separated. It was a repetition of yesterday's nightmare.

As we rushed on, the air was filled with a smell so sickening that it burned its way into every fiber of my being and brought a wave of nausea over me. We soon discovered that the source of this terrible odor was the corpse of a young pregnant women, her body swollen and turning blackish green. Her eyes were locked open in an expression of utter horror. Although my parents rushed us past her body, I found my gaze was irresistibly drawn to hers causing a wave of sickness that welled up from the pit of my stomach and turned my legs to rubber.

We were constantly being urged by our parents to hold on to one another to avoid being separated. Fatigue and hunger overcame us much earlier on the second day, but still we walked on, eating as we walked. Papa urged us to move even faster since we were now approaching the outskirts of the city, and, at this pace, by nightfall we would be into the country-side.

I was puzzled by his insistence that we travel this far from the city, since the Khmer Rouge kept telling us we would be allowed to return in a few days. But I believe by now Papa knew that this was simply another trick to enhance the coop-eration of the people. As we continued on, the crowds began to thin out and we were able to move faster. By 5:30, we reached the suburbs of Phnom Penh. As the refugees began to fan out into the countryside each family searched for some sign of shelter. We soon learned that the people from the vil-lages outside of the capital had also been forced to leave. The town's shops were abandoned and no food or shelter was available. Those families that had failed to bring food were now desperate. One man was screaming to the crowds offer-ing huge piles of currency for food. His hysteria quickly increased as he stood by the roadside pleading with anyone to sell him their food. There were no takers. Just before night-fall, we came upon a small house in the middle of a grove of coconut, mango, and orange trees. Papa approached the resi-dence to ask for assistance but this house, too, was abandoned. That night we slept under the trees next to this small cottage.

The morning came and with it, once again the harsh, angry voices of the Khmer Rouge ordering us to continue on the road. By now, our own supply of food was almost gone and the sense of hunger began to replace our fear and confusion. Fortunately, we shortly came upon an abandoned vegetable garden which miraculously had not been discovered by other refugees. With renewed strength, we all ran as fast as we could into the garden and picked as much food as we could possibly carry.

At the end of the day, the Khmer Rouge finally informed us that we could not return to the city and that, in fact, we must travel as far from the capital as possible under threat of death. At that point my parents decided that we would proceed to Papa's hometown of Kampong Cham where his mother still lived. Although this was a considerable distance away, it seemed to be a safe destination. By evening, we reached another village and finally stopped walking. We chose a spot near a large lake to spend the night and came upon a field of sweet potatoes. We thanked God for providing us with enough food to take on our journey. It had been three days since we were forced to leave our home and bathing in the cool refreshing waters of the lake at least temporarily erased the memories of the horrors we had experienced.

We stayed that night in the abandoned village, the streets empty and deserted; a ghost town left to its own devices.

At about 5:00 a.m. the next morning, a group of Khmer Rouge woke us and ordered us to start moving again. Within an hour we were on the road, joining other refugees, but at least now, we had a destination. Even though it might take many days to reach Kampong Cham, there was something to look forward to.

Early the next morning we started our journey to Papa's house, a trip that would ultimately take about a month. Each day now fell into a routine; walking all day, stopping only to eat and continuing again until dark when we looked for a grove of trees where we would spend the night. The long march, often undertaken with long periods of silence, gave me much time to sort out my thoughts which centered largely on my family. As was true for most of the refugees, we searched constantly for those family members with whom we had lost contact, especially my grandmother and my uncle on my mother's side, my oldest brother, Choeun, who, as far as we knew, was still in Battdambang when we were forced to evacuate, and my brother, Thouch, who had left for Battdambang just before the Khmer Rouge captured Phnom Penh. In the case of my paternal grandmother in Kampong Cham, I hadn't seen her since I was a small child and the prospect of seeing her again when we got to Papa's house filled me with great anticipation. The last word we had was that she had survived the fighting and was still living in the house where Papa grew up. From time to time as we walked, I also contemplated on how quickly my life and the lives of my people were changing. Needless to say, these thoughts were overwhelming to a child of nine.

2

The trip to my grandmother's house took about three weeks during which time each day brought with it fatigue and hunger. My feet were swollen with blisters and each step was painful. We bathed only rarely when we came upon a lake or stream. Once, I waded into a lake up to my waist and suddenly stepped into a deep hole that had been caused by a bomb. Before I could cry out, my head was under water and I surely would have drowned except for a stranger who was nearby washing his clothes. He rushed to my assistance, grabbed me by my hair and pulled me out of the water coughing and shaking.

Finally, we came to a small town that was a day's journey from Kampong Cham where we spent the night. I looked forward to our reunion with my grandmother with hope and the next morning we started toward the town that had been home to Papa and, we thought, was still home to my grandmother. As we continued on, Papa met up with some of his old friends who gave him news of his mother. They also warned him that the Khmer Rouge were questioning and searching everyone, investigating, in particular, anyone tied to the prior government or to outside influences. In our case, there were any number of circumstances that would arouse suspicion or, even worse, cause us harm. Papa had been a government employee and this fact alone would result in his execution. Moreover, my second brother, Thom, had served in the military and he was still carrying his old army uniform wrapped in a blanket. My mother was also carrying Thom's helicopter mechanic certificate and three other certificates which he had brought back with him from America. If they found any of these possessions we would all be in jeopardy. We immediately threw anything that we considered to be of risk into the river which was near at hand except for Thom's certificates which we buried by a bamboo bush.

While we were just outside of Kampong Cham, Chantha and her fiancee Samouth, informed us that they had decided not to wait any longer and they were married in the open countryside in a brief ceremony. We all would have wanted a proper marriage, but they were very much in love and uncertain when a more appropriate occasion would arrive.

By late afternoon, we were close to my grandmother's house. We had joined up with a group of perhaps 25 other refugee families who had also arrived at Kampong Cham in search of loved ones. As we walked through the streets, the local residents stood out in front of their homes and stared at us with expressions of naked hostility as if we too were their enemy. Their cold, quiet anger made me fear for our lives. Again, questions too complex for a child to answer formed in my mind. Why would strangers who knew nothing of us hate us?

We finally reached my grandmother's house and saw her standing outside as word of our arrival had reached her earlier. Papa rushed to her and they clutched each other in a tight embrace, too overcome with emotion to engage in conversation. After what seemed like an eternity Papa turned to us with tears in his eyes and my grandmother stood there smiling at us with open arms. I saw her just as I remembered her years ago. We ran to her and she held us with all of the love she could muster.

There is no telling how long we would have remained that way, happy that we all had survived the terror and the nightmare of the past month. However, our joy was abruptly interrupted by the arrival of six Khmer Rouge soldiers who ordered us to turn over our possessions for their inspection. Just as we had been warned earlier, they searched our few belongings that still remained and we were left with our own private thoughts, imagining what would have happened if they had discovered my brother's old army uniform or anything that would have associated Papa as a government employee.

The thought raced through my mind that they would discover something we had overlooked which would result in our harm, and I trembled in fear as they continued poking through our belongings. After completing their search, they entered my grandmother's house to continue their investigation. We were not allowed to enter until they had confiscated what they wanted and left with their usual threats.

As soon as they departed, we rushed into the house and gathered around my grandmother to catch up on the last five years when we had lost regular contact with one another. As exhausted as we were from our long journey, not one of us fell asleep that night as we listened in utter amazement and pride as she told us how she had survived the fighting which at the time was fierce in that part of Cambodia. She was then 79 years old and a tribute to her courage and patience. As we listened to her account, we forgot the tragedy and sorrows of our own experiences.

The joy we shared at renewing our love and support with

my grandmother was short-lived. We were soon to discover the true magnitude of life under the Khmer Rouge regime.

Early the next morning, three men appeared at my grandmother's house claiming to be the town managers and ordering us to attend a meeting that was shortly to take place in the center of town. Their demeanor was so menacing that we were struck with fear as to the purpose of the meeting. When we arrived at the appointed place we joined with all of the other recent arrivals to Kampong Cham. We stood in stark contrast to the Khmer Rouge in their black uniforms, ordering and shouting instructions. Shortly after our arrival, their leader mounted a podium and with little formality, described the terms of our existence under their rule. We were the new people in town and we needed to be reeducated if we were to be accepted into the community. Our reeducation would begin by having us cast off all of our ancient customs in favor of revolutionary values. No longer, for example, could we refer to our parents as Papa and Ma, since these were symbols of a decadent tradition. Instead all parents were to be addressed as *Bok* and *My* to signify the changed status of family relationships. The new order was to be addressed as *Angka*, that is the organization or the cooperative that would replace the family as the central influence in our lives. We would begin our new lives by working in the fields surrounding the village. By our labor, we would learn the true meaning of communism or Angka. We were dismissed with instructions to return tomorrow to the same meeting place prepared to work.

We returned to my grandmother's house puzzled and concerned over how these developments would change our lives. One thing was apparent. For whatever reasons, Angka considered us to be their enemy and this sentiment was shared by the townspeople who continued to express their hostility toward us. Even the childhood friends of the man I loved as Papa and must now call Bok turned their backs on him, some of them openly expressing their envy because we had enjoyed a better life than they had. We were to see this same strategy over and over: turn one group against another, play on people's basic fears and prejudices, and in this fashion, divide and conquer. As these various circumstances became clearer to me, I resolved to restrain myself from any open expression of anger or frustration. I gradually came to realize that the best way to cope with such experiences was to accept the loss of external freedom and control. No matter how much I might hate how these events changed others, I would not allow them to change my basic values and my own private feelings. In that manner I would maintain some degree of inner or private control over my own destiny.

The next morning came all too soon and we marched to the town center along with all of the other families who had been given similar instructions: here again, we quickly learned another of Angka's strategies. All of these new adult women, including My (my mom's new title), were forced to work with the adult women of the village. Similarly, Bok went off with the men and older boys. My two brothers, Thoeun and Than, were instructed to work with the boys of the village and my sister, Chan, and I were grouped with 50 other recently arrived young girls, none of whom we knew. We were assigned to work in a corn field with them which was about two miles from my grandmother's house.

This arrangement was also by design since, as we shortly discovered, the local children who had already been converted to Angka ostracized us from their group. It is in the nature of children to want to be accepted by their peers and, in this fashion, we too would fall under the influence of Angka.

Since neither one of us had any prior experience of field work, that first day was unbearable for us. The physical labor, husking the corn, carrying it in huge heavy baskets under intense heat, with no shoes to protect our feet was almost beyond endurance. When added to the primitive working conditions, I wondered if I would survive that first day. We were allowed to stop to eat only for a few minutes at a time. When we got thirsty, the only water available was the river which was also used by the entire town for a variety of purposes including bathing and drinking by the farmers' livestock. When I could no longer resist the need and I bent down to drink from the river, I was briefly overcome with the sense that perhaps this was simply a horrible nightmare. My need for water quickly brought me back to the real world of Angka tyranny. This, too, was part of their plan—to strip us of our dignity and self-respect and to teach us humility as they understood it.

3

Over the next several months our new lives in Kampong Cham became reality and our earlier existence in Phnom Penh faded into mere memory. Perhaps the most demanding adjustment we had to make to our new circumstances was to cope with what we slowly and painfully came to recognize as a planned, systematic effort to starve us into submission. At the beginning of each month, we received a small portion of rice and corn and a portion of salt. This was to last until the next food distribution 30 days later. Although we worked every day in the fields, planting and harvesting rice, beans, sugar cane and vegetables, taking any food for one's own personal use led to beatings or worse. The only additional food source allowed was fish from a nearby lake if they were caught before the work day began. In this fashion each day passed with monotonous regularity and even those of us who were children accepted the one common reality—one must work to stay alive. Any departure from this fundamental principle would result in either delayed starvation or immediate execution.

After three months, we had all changed in both small and dramatic ways. In my case, my hands and feet developed hardened callouses. Although I learned to live with the physical pain, I hated the other changes our new lifestyle forced on me. Long hair was a custom and a source of pride among

Cambodian girls, but the lack of soap and clean water, and the ever-present lice and fleas made this impossible. Sooner or later we found it easier and more sanitary to keep our hair short. Again, the impact of this change was personally humiliating to all of us since we felt that we were betraying our traditions. The threat of disease was also of constant concern and we regularly searched for the tell-tale changes in skin color which signified the presence of hepatitis.

We also soon discovered that Angka agents, known to us as *Chhlop*, were everywhere in our midst and that any semblance of privacy and trust were also memories of the past. After the end of the workday when families gathered together to share their meager provisions and personal thoughts, any discussion or expression which might be interpreted as critical of the new regime would lead to an arrest of the offending parties. The typical practice was for Chhlop to appear at a suspect's house, usually at night, and announce that he was to be reeducated. He was then taken into the jungle never to be seen again. After several such incidents, our conversations became hushed and restricted to a few safe topics. Above and beyond these harsh circumstances, Angka never missed an opportunity to belittle or humiliate us. If one of us became too ill to work, we became the target of abuse even if we ran a high fever or suffered from other obvious physical symptoms. This despite the fact that we were close to starvation and were denied even the most basic sanitary facilities which caused us to become physically weaker and more easily prone to disease. And always we were reminded of our status as enemies of the people, as parasites of the working class, as exploiters of others.

If we thought that our conditions had reached rock bottom, we were constantly discovering that Angka could still make matters worse. Our rice ration, for example, was constantly being reduced to the point where our basic staple was rice soup since we could add enough water and plant leaves for everyone in the family. Unfortunately, the nourishing value of such fare was clearly minimal.

There were other indignities too numerous to mention. Suffice it to say that I was a nine-year old with now, little reason to believe that my life would ever be different. It was work or starve, and so I, along with my family and the others who shared our condition, continued in this manner, day after day, carrying on our lives as best as we could.

4

After about five months since our arrival in Kampong Cham, my older sister, Chantha, learned that her mother-in-law was alive and living two towns away. Much to our surprise, Angka granted her request for her and her husband to join his mother. We were all saddened by their departure, but at least this circumstance offered some hope that their lives would be better than if they continued to live with us in Kampong Cham. We heard no more from them despite many efforts to learn of their circumstances. It seemed that our family circle was gradually diminishing. Was this also by design?

We lived in this manner for about another four months, constantly tired from our physical labors, weakened by the bare subsistence level of food and, perhaps most desperately, living in fear that any day Angka would detain my father because of his employment by the former regime. Every day, one or more men were arrested and led away because they had been government workers or in the military or even simply because they were professionals. We were all encouraged to act in a confident manner since the slightest expression of concern over our prior identity could bring the focus of attention on us and our father.

Another four months passed in this manner with long moments of unendurable monotony, fatigue and routine, punctuated intermittently by moments of terror. One morning, without warning Angka arrived at my grandmother's house and informed us with no further word that we must pack our things and be prepared to move in two days.

This message struck terror in our hearts. No matter how miserable our current status, at least we had each other and we knew that we could not endure any further suffering, especially if we were separated. My mother was particularly concerned that we would be leaving without informing Chantha, and she pleaded with the local people to get word to her of our being forced to leave. The morning of our departure came when we had to leave my grandmother behind. She had pleaded with Angka to allow her to accompany us, but they were unyielding in their cruelty to this elderly woman whose only concern was for her family. My last recollection of her was this tragic figure who, in the short time of our reacquaintance, I had come to love with all my heart. She was standing in the doorway, tears on her face waving goodbye. We kept turning back to look and to wave, shouting our love; all except my father, who was crying disconsolately. His tears flowed freely, the only time during our trials that he lost emotional control.

As we were being marched out of town, we pleaded with the people we recognized as my grandmother's friends to watch after her and to inform her that we would get word to her as soon as we reached our destination. The only problem with that was that we had no idea where we were being taken nor what our future would portend.

Once again, we fell into a familiar pattern. Groups of families walking silently together, parents clutching the hands of their children, most of us imagining the worst. About 2:00 that afternoon we arrived at a river site where five large unsafe-looking boats were at berth. There were about 20 or 30 families in the group and when we reached the dock, Angka was on the boats ordering us to board. The scene was nightmarish. Men in black uniforms threatening all of us with their weapons, hurling insults, women and children screaming with terror, and all of us herded out onto the boats. Each boat was crammed to its capacity, and we grabbed at one another so as not to fall over the side. My heart was pounding in my chest from fright.

Finally, everyone was loaded onto the boats and as we pulled away from the shore, I thought of my grandmother, her face wet with tears and I, too, started to cry.

The journey by boat was long and tiresome. We were forced to sit the entire time for fear that the boat would capsize if we stood up. We had been traveling down river for many hours with no inkling as to our destination. At one point, I heard one of the Angka soldiers say that we were going through Phnom Penh on the MeKong River and my heart leaped with joy at the prospect of returning to my beloved home.

But we merely passed by the capital and our view of what was once one of the most beautiful cities in Southeast Asia left me with despair. The city was without lights and virtually devoid of any sign of humanity. Buildings and trees had been leveled and replaced by a totally ruined landscape. In less than a year, a city of a thousand years was reduced to rubble. We were all sick with sadness. Why was it necessary to destroy everything, even if you believed that the new regime was committed to rebuilding a new country?

The next day, our situation was becoming desperate. We had been this entire time with little or no food or water and frightened beyond our wits at not knowing what was in store. Finally, Angka told us that our destination was Battdambang which we would reach by about 6:00 that night.

The news that we were going to Battdambang jarred us as if we had been struck dumb. This was the town that my brother, Thouch, had gone to just before Angka had invaded Phnom Penh. As far as we knew, my oldest brother, Choeun, and his family still lived there and now, after a year of silence perhaps we would be reunited. After all of the disappointments and the continuing decline of our lifestyles, this was almost too much to hope for.

That evening, we reached a small village on the outskirts of Battdambang and joined up with thousands of others, brought here from all over Cambodia. We searched among the crowd for signs of a familiar face but learned only that the city of Battdambang had also been evacuated, at the same time as Phnom Penh. Now, once again, we were left to wonder if my brothers were still alive.

As night approached, we began to search for a suitable sleeping arrangement, which now meant the outdoors as a matter of routine. We finally found shelter away from the crowds under a large tree. Given the trying time we had experienced over the last several days our only thought was for sleep. However, just as we had completed our preparations, we noticed several Angka soldiers looking at us in a curious way. This was most alarming and struck terror in our hearts since we had learned that one could best achieve safety through anonymity. It was Angka's practice to focus their hostility on anyone who stood out from the crowd. And so we tried to remain calm and deliberate while sneaking furtive glances in their direction. Finally, our hearts stopped as we noticed that they were clearly walking toward us, and there was no question of their intent. They walked directly up to my father and instructed him to follow them. This was the moment we dreaded since we had witnessed this same scene repeated many times, often ending with the targeted person never being seen again.

As they led my father a short distance away from us, my mother's face turned white and she clutched us to her, all of us fearing the worst. No one spoke, but we were trembling with fear for our father.

We continued to watch as they stopped to talk with him. We were unable to hear any of the discussion but we could easily see their angry gestures and their confrontational attitude. Whatever my father was being accused of, we could discern from their reactions that they did not believe his explanation.

They gestured for him to follow them into a wooded area and now, as they vanished from sight, it seemed that whatever little hope we had that he would be spared was to be abandoned. I began to cry uncontrollably, huge sobs racking my body. I was totally convinced that my beloved father who had been so kind, understanding and strong throughout our ordeal was about to leave our lives forever.

I sank to the ground, crying for what seemed like an eternity, but in fact, was probably no more than several minutes. My heart pounded in my chest and I felt that there was no longer any reason to live.

Finally, the soldiers emerged from the woods with my father walking behind them. I cried with even greater intensity out of relief and joy at seeing that he was still alive. When the group approached us, my father said nothing but walked directly to my mother and asked her to hand over a small radio that she had been carrying. Apparently, this entire incident centered on the fact that Angka merely wanted the radio and my father's watch. As he walked past us to hand them over, my father whispered in my ear that everything would be all right and that I should stop crying. With no further word, he handed them the radio and the watch and they left in silence. When they were out of sight, we collectively breathed a huge sigh of relief, and I consciously tried to stop my body from trembling. We were safe again for a while, but who knew how long it would be before the next confrontation?

The next morning we woke still physically and emotionally drained from last night's ordeal. My mother was already up and she informed us that she was now going to search for Thouch and Choeun. She promptly walked off, moving through the crowds, asking everyone she met if they had any news of their whereabouts. At about noon, she returned to where we were resting. The broad smile across her face told us she was bringing us good news. She had encountered a man she recognized as Choeun's neighbor, and he had informed her that both brothers had gone to the town of *Ksour* that was about 16 hours away.

We all rejoiced in the news but we also recognized that Angka would probably not allow us to leave Battdambang. Nevertheless, my father resolved to ask for permission and he went off in search of the men who had confronted us last night, reasoning that they might be more inclined to grant his request than any of the others. He returned shortly and told us that they would permit only my mother and my brother, Than, to make the trip. The rest of us would have to remain here outside Battdambang. My father had mixed emotions about this plan. Although he desperately wanted us all to be reunited, there were also unknown risks to be taken into account, since a good part of the journey was through thick jungle. My mother, however, was adamant and she dismissed his fears with a wave of her hand. Now that Angka had granted permission she was determined to have her family reunited and nothing would stand in her way.

My mother and Than started on their journey early the next morning. I knew I would miss her terribly and we all prayed for their safety. As each day passed with no news, we became increasingly concerned about their welfare. Even under the present circumstances, their trip should not have taken more than two days, so after five days had passed, we were now getting very anxious. My father kept up a brave front and constantly reassured us but we were beginning to fear the worst. Around mid-day, as we searched down the road that my mother and brother had taken, two familiar figures began to emerge from the forest. My heart leaped with joy as I recognized my two brothers, Thouch and Choeun, walking toward us. We rushed to one another and embraced them, flooding them with questions. They told us that my mother and Than had made the journey safely and that they had arrived two days earlier and were going to remain in Ksour while we joined up with them.

My oldest brother, Choeun, had been given permission to bring us back to them where we would all be together again for the first time since the revolution. The only one missing from our immediate family would now be my sister, Chantha, who was still living with her in-laws. Although this was a troubling circumstance, my family and Savvy's family decided that we would leave the camp we were in early the next morning.

But first, we were so overjoyed at the prospect of all of us having survived the past year's terrible ordeal, we talked late into
the night, reviewing our experiences with my brothers and
cautiously planning for the future.

We started out the next day, all 19 of us, including in-laws,
I thought about how our circumstances continued to change
so quickly and almost always by happenstance. Out of about
280 families that lived in the refugee camp with us near
Battdambang, to my knowledge, we were the only families
allowed to leave. Four years later we learned that, shortly after
we had departed this camp, Angka had executed all of the
refugees in the camp. This, of course, was only one of the
many mass murders that they committed, and the faces of the
people we came to know, in this camp, especially the women
and children, haunt me to this day.

5

Once again now, we were walking to an unknown future although, at least this time, except for Chantha, our entire family would be together. The journey through the jungle was extremely exhausting because of the intense heat which pressed in on us from all sides. In addition, there were no roads, only a hard and cruel jungle trail. Nevertheless, we walked as fast as possible because of our fear of meeting Angka patrols and not knowing how they would deal with us if we encountered them.

Darkness came quickly and by now we were all exhausted, thirsty, and frightened. The only sounds of life were the birds calling from the trees and the insects buzzing around our heads. Despite these difficulties, Choeun urged us to walk even faster since he planned on our arriving at Ksour that evening.

It was late that night by the time we reached our destination. Because of the almost complete darkness, it was impossible to see much of anything. My brother had told us that this was actually an abandoned rural community surrounded by areas cleared for farming. Nevertheless, about 200 to 300 people had taken refuge here.

Finally, we reached my brother's house which turned out to be no more than a one-room hut built a with a palm-leaf roof.

Once again, we slept outdoors which by now was our customary routine. When we woke the next morning and looked around the area we saw little sign of permanent human residence, just open fields with a few large trees and the temporary huts that served as shelters for other families. We also learned that the water supply consisted of a small pond a short distance away which was dirty and overgrown with weeds. At one time, what seemed now another lifetime ago, we would have rejected the mere thought of drinking from such a source. Extreme thirst, however, has a way of inducing one to drink anything.

We spent the next morning building our own hut and trying to catch up on lost time. We had barely scratched the surface, reviewing our experiences when once again, we were interrupted by two Angka guards who instructed us in our "new" responsibilities. It was a pattern with which we were already too familiar.

The first night that we spent in our own hut was a time of reflection for me. Although in some ways I was happy that our family was together again, my emotions were mixed. I remember the anger and sadness and confusion that I also experienced over the actions of Angka. Why were they killing innocent people, causing so much suffering and creating an atmosphere of terror? My last thoughts before falling asleep were of my hatred for Angka.

Early the next day we were once again forced into work sections just as we had been over a year ago in Kampong Cham. This time, however, we were separated into various groups. My two brothers, Thouch and Thom, joined other young men who would be required to do the most physically demanding tasks. They were marched off with no further word regarding their destination, how long they would be gone or if we were to ever see them again.

All the younger children including my sister Chan and my sister-in-law Savvy's younger sisters Vanna and Sony, and I were required to attend the communist school at the center of town for one to two hours each morning. There were no chairs or tables so we all sat on the ground and listened to the Angka instructor indoctrinating us into their beliefs. This was an uneducated cruel woman of about 20 years old. We later learned that it was common practice by Angka to use criminals for such purposes since they were easily controlled and could be relied on to say only what the communists wanted them to say. For some reason, the four of us were singled out by her and the other students as particular targets for their abuse in part because of our light complexion. We were told that we were not allowed to leave the town or to own any utensils except for one plate and a spoon. Our meals were to be eaten in a common guarded area and mealtimes were signaled by three rings of a bell which occurred twice a day, midday and at night. We were each given the same amount of food and whatever was not eaten was to be returned to Angka. We were particularly warned against trying to bring any food back to our hut.

That first day of the new routine, while marching to the indoctrination area from our meal, I saw the adults returning from the fields for their meal. My heart wrenched when I saw my mother and father, covered with dirt and mud, exhausted and bent from a day of hard physical labor out in the harsh, unyielding sun. It was crippling to me to see how they had been sapped of all their strength and I wanted to reach out to comfort and hold them. But we were now being marched out to the fields ourselves where we were forced to work the rest of the day and into the night planting potatoes.

Even though my body was now hardened to the rigors of such labors, the undergrowth in this part of Cambodia was particularly harsh and I had to struggle with all of my strength to keep up with the others.

Somehow, I managed to continue working until the bell rang again and we were finally marched back to town for our evening meal. I saw my father in line with the other men and I knew that our ration, a small scoop of rice and a small cup of vegetables in hot water would not even begin to meet his needs in his weakened state. So I made it a point to save some for his plate. That night when we returned to our small hut we made a candle from fish fat and a long thin piece of cloth. As we sat there in silence, and I saw the tired faces of my parents with deep furrows on their brows, I was overcome with a great sense of despair. The good and happy life of my childhood stood in stark contrast to our present circumstances—a meager fragile hut with palm leaves served as our home, lit by fish fat. Our circumstances now were perhaps even more bleak than what we had experienced in Kampong Cham. I fell into a restless sleep with one thought—will my family and I survive this nightmare?

Over the next several days, our routine seldom varied. Up early to attend the meeting for our education into the glories of communism and then to the fields. On most occasions we planted crops and watered them from buckets filled at a distant swamp carried on a harness across our shoulders. On other occasions we gathered firewood for the cooks. This was particularly difficult for my sister and me since we had never experienced any work of this type before. On such occasions, we were marched into the jungle through heavy brush, gather an armful of wood into a large bundle with our bare hands and carry it back to the cooking site on our heads. This chore was repeated throughout the entire day so that by nightfall we had been sapped of every ounce of strength in our bodies. Each day at mealtime I searched out my father and tried to convince him that I had more than enough food for myself and to get him to eat some portion of my ration. Very quickly, however, he saw through this pretense and refused my offering. His reassurances that I must stay strong to survive and that he would be all right always brought tears to my eyes. I realized, once again, how much we loved one another and that my father would literally sacrifice his life for his children.

As our hunger increased, many of us began to forage for food in the jungle. On one occasion, Chan, Vanna, Sony and I came across a cluster of berries which we ate in one sitting out of desperation. Two days later, Sony became very ill, vomiting and running a high fever. Within the next several days, her condition deteriorated, and her family carried her to the Angka hospital. Vanna went to see her the next day and returned to us in a state of shock. Sony was so terribly ill that she was literally passing her insides out through her mouth. The next time her family went to see her, her body had been removed and was buried in a mass grave along with the other hospital victims.

About a week after Sony died, our group was informed that we were to work in the rice fields behind the women's group. I thought immediately that this might be an opportunity for me to see my mother. As we marched out to the field, we could see the women in the distance bent over with their sickles, cutting the rice that surrounded the paddies. Our job was to gather the rice into bunches and then move the bunches to a central location. It was again hard, exhausting work in the constant hot sun and after working for hours that first day, I was beginning to feel weak and dizzy. My feet had swelled from the rough ground and my body started to itch all over from contact with the rough stalks and the incessant insects. My legs were covered with a rash and I felt that I could not continue, but I saw others drop from exhaustion who were never to be seen again. It was a matter of pure, basic survival at which point one's mind becomes numb to the pain and the discomfort and the body continues to respond almost automatically. By evening, I was almost in a trance when I heard the whistle of Angka signaling the end of work and a return to the eating place. Despite my pain, the hope that I might see my mother filled me with great anticipation but once we arrived she was nowhere to be seen.

Our meal that evening consisted of a small portion of rice and a small salted fish. It was apparent to me once again, that Angka were implementing a systematic starvation program.

The next evening, after we returned from another 13 hours of hard labor in the hot sun with no rest, I saw my mother at the eating place. We talked about our experiences and I told her that I was working in the field next to her. She was pleased to hear this, but we said nothing about our physical condition. Any comments that could be interpreted as a complaint or a sign of weakness was reported to authorities with dire consequences. However, my mother quietly managed to inform me that Angka were conducting a serious search for anyone connected with the prior government or military and that if asked, I was to say that my father had driven a taxi before the revolution and that my brother, Thom, had worked in a gas station. Obviously, we were being prepared for an interrogation and this insured that our stories would be consistent.

Again, I was reminded that our survival hinged on the merest thread of coincidence. Several days later, I was indeed asked about my father's occupation before Angka overthrew the government and I answered as my mother instructed. Those children who said that their fathers were professionals, such as teachers, doctors, government workers and so forth were unwittingly responsible for their fathers' executions.

Once again, our lives fell into a familiar routine. The work requirements continued to escalate while our rations continued to decrease. Moreover, our water supply was a dirty and insect-infested swamp about a mile distant from our camp. Here, we also had to contest with leaches and poisonous snakes. Occasionally, I would discover that a leech had become attached to my body, throwing me into a state of panic. I would scream and struggle to remove it which left me with a terror that exists to the present time. As we were too frightened to bathe under such circumstances, our personal hygiene also began to deteriorate. With all of these factors disease and death became commonplace. It is impossible to calculate the number of men, women and children who lost their lives in just this one brutal camp in Cambodia.

6

Spring came and the season which was always celebrated for its joyful qualities only deepened the misery of those of us in the town. The heavy rains, so necessary for the rice crop left us covered with mud every day. We would sink to our knees as we planted the rice and this, together with the cold and dampness, left our clothes constantly wet and in rags. As the season progressed, my lips turned purple and my arms and legs shrank to less than two inches thick. By this point in time our entire daily meal consisted of a tablespoon of rice and a cup of boiled water. It was almost impossible to distinguish between those of us who were near death and those who had actually succumbed. It seemed as if almost everyone was indifferent to the question of life or death. Still my parents urged us on, offering hope, challenging us to stay alive. Then the day came when Angka announced their next plan for those of us who had managed to survive. All the residents in the camp were to work under separate assignments, with the men being transported deep into the jungle, while the children were to set up their own camp some distance away from what was now the women's quarters.

This news left me terrified beyond belief. Despite all of the hardships that I had endured up to this point, at least I always knew that I would return at the end of the day to the arms of my mother. Now my heart was broken and the will to survive was gone. I was ten years old and convinced that I would not live to my eleventh birthday.

The next morning, Angka came for us at 6 a.m. There was no time for extended goodbyes or expressions of any sentiment. My only possessions were two pairs of pants and two tops. One moment I was in the embrace of my mother and the next moment I was completely alone in the company of strangers being led to an uncertain future. As I left her arms, she thrust a piece of black plastic in my bag. We walked all that day with one brief stop and arrived at our new encampment late in the afternoon. I was in a stupor throughout the entire day, scarcely aware of my companions or my surroundings.

We were guarded by two middle-aged women who informed us that we would remain in this camp until December or January when the rice season ended. Despite our fatigue and emotional state, they ordered us to remove the brush to make a clearing for our sleeping quarters. We finally completed the task late that evening only to discover that 10 other girls would also be sharing the clearing with us. Huddled together, distraught over our circumstances, frightened at the uncertainty of our future, we spent our first night in the jungle, with only a small cotton net only partially protecting us from the mosquitos, and whatever else might represent a threat to us.

That night, lying in total darkness, it seemed like my body was numb and detached. I listened to the peaceful sounds of the birds in the trees, but, more close at hand, the other girls crying out of fright and hunger was a much starker reality. I was beyond crying myself.

I looked up into the darkening sky as if searching in my despair in the depths of the heavens. The stars shone with unusual brilliance and the round, full moon seemed to offer a sign of warmth and sympathy. I began talking to it as if it was a loved one who was there to comfort me. Finally, I fell asleep, consoled in the light of the moon. It was an experience that soon became a regular practice and which was to see me through many lonely nights.

We were awakened very early the next morning and as I looked around to orient myself, I saw that a married women's group had camped not too far from our quarters. The women were living under the same conditions as we were. To my surprise and delight, my sister-in-law, Savvy, was one of the women in the group. She looked as we all did; tired, dazed and hungry. Shortly thereafter, Angka gave us our instructions. We were told that the name of the camp was *Krorbow*, a crude site cleared out of the jungle and home to thick clouds of insects that would descend on us every evening. We were given long sharp knives and ordered to cut down all of the small trees and shrubs, bundle them and carry them to a central clearing. A huge fire was set and a thick black cloud of smoke immediately filled the air, searing into our lungs and causing us to cough and choke. While we were attempting to recover and with no further delay, we were marched to the designated area and began our exhausting labor, still coughing and choking. We stopped for nothing, but continued into the evening when we received one bowl of rice soup.

After several days, most of us were in a desperate situation, bordering on starvation. Many of the girls would sneak off into the brush and eat anything they caught that might provide some source of nourishment including snakes, toads, and dead birds. This was a dangerous act since it could lead to punishment and even execution. Moreover, I had learned from Sony's experience how risky this was.

I was getting sicker with each passing day. There was virtually no muscle left on my body at all, just skin and bones. My head was bigger than my trunk even though my body was swollen from starvation. Soon I became feverish, my eyes started swelling and I lost my vision. I knew then I was on the threshold of death. I wanted to die, I was ready for it, yet the thought of dying without my mother was my greatest fear. I was left in this condition by the two women guards who had seen this same circumstance many times. Even if they were inclined to offer assistance, there was no medicine available so I would either die like the others or heal myself naturally. I remained motionless, unfed, and suffering for perhaps a week.

Then, for some unknown reason, the fever broke, my eyesight gradually returned, and I slowly recovered. I learned that many of the children had experienced the same symptoms which apparently was due to an allergy to something in the jungle. Many of those of us who had been ill died and I wondered if those of us who had lived through this nightmare were really the fortunate ones.

We worked in this area of the jungle for about a month enduring incredible hardships. The death rate was increasing rapidly and every night was punctuated by the screaming and moaning of those who were in the final stages of starvation. Finally, even Angka took note of the astounding death rate and we were told that we would be returning to *Ksour*. There was great hope among the survivors that our return would bring with it an improvement in our food supply, but when we emerged from the jungle and entered the town, we learned that many of the people who had remained behind had also died of starvation. This was, in fact, a town of living dead. Everyone I met, including my own family members was in the last stages of starvation. The sight of my father was even more shocking than when I had last seen him. He was now completely bald, and his body shrunk to half its size. The change was so striking that it left me speechless. No doubt, my appearance was equally appalling to him and my mother. I had no fat on my body at all. My ribs were pushing out of my chest, my arms reduced to sticks covered with skin, and I was so weak I could barely walk without stumbling. Many of the babies who were born at Ksour during this time died either at birth or shortly thereafter. Those mothers who needed any kind of assistance at childbirth also died, since there were no medical personnel or medications available to treat them. My 18-month old niece, Karin, who had been born to Choeun and Kim Run during our evacuation had been left under my mother's care while they were forced to work in other camps. When I saw her condition, I was convinced that she would die within a week. She was totally moribund, unable to move or speak. Flies gathered around her face because of her lack of movement. She seemed completely oblivious to her environment and to her own needs. Only my mother refused to accept the obvious, and she would literally force food down the child's throat. In this manner, Karin somehow managed to survive through this desperate time, and gradually grew stronger. I cannot say for certain, but my best estimate is that perhaps 30% of the residents of Ksour died of starvation over the next several weeks. I remember, in particular, the screams of an elderly man who begged for food almost constantly over a five-day period. Gradually he grew weaker until the screaming finally ended. There was no one able to help him and all we could think of was when we would meet a similar fate.

Despite our terrible circumstances, those of us who could still move were forced to continue to work in the fields, except, now, we were reduced to an even more primitive level of survival. Whenever possible, we would search the jungle for anything that might provide nourishment—leaves, weeds, mushrooms, frogs, and snakes, in fact anything that might hold off starvation for another day. We learned what was safe and what was not safe by watching the reactions of others, for example, someone dying of poisonous mushrooms. The death rate was so rapid and our resources so meager that each day bodies were simply carried off to be scattered through the jungle later to be buried in shallow graves.

Of course, Angka never lacked food for themselves, often leaving any extras to spoil rather than share it with their captives. Occasionally, people were driven to barter personal possessions such as gold and diamonds for a piece of chicken. My mother had long ago traded almost all of her jewelry and now, with almost nothing left of value, we were virtually helpless. In this state, some parents resorted to stealing food from Angka for their children which, of course, involved the ultimate risk. On one occasion a man was caught stealing a potato from Angka supplies. He was immediately taken to a tree in the center of the town where he was tied and whipped mercilessly as an example for the rest of us. The whipping continued for several days when he was finally released, only to die a few days later.

By the end of 1976 I, like everyone else, was a walking skeleton. But for those of us who thought that our lives could not be any more desperate, we were to find the worst was yet to come.

Shortly thereafter, I developed terrible stomach pains which caused me to double up and scream in agony. Two days passed in this manner in which I was unable to even move. Then, I felt an itch in my throat and I began to choke. I started to cough as I hard as I could and, to my horror, I started to expel live round worms from my nose and throat. My stomach began to swell as I began to excrete the worms. I thought my body was literally exploding—a feeling I shall never forget. At this point I was convinced that I was going to die.

As horrified as my mother was, she now knew what was wrong and the proper treatment for this condition. She decided to plead with Angka for the necessary medication to clear my body of the worms. For barter, she offered a guard her gold wedding ring which she somehow had managed to retain as one of her last precious possessions.

When she returned with the medicine, my oldest brother, Choeun, who had managed to bury one syringe from his pharmacy, inserted the medication into the syringe and injected it directly into my abdomen four times. The reaction was almost immediate. The pain increased unbearably as the worms were activated and made their way out of my body. I was terrified at the sight and doubled over with pain. Almost as quickly, however, the pain subsided and I started to feel relief.

As I began to recover, my mother helped me up and walked with me into the jungle where I passed the remaining dead worms. Although I was still weak and dizzy with exhaustion and terror, I began to feel better just knowing that this incredible ordeal was behind me.

7

Although I was still in a weakened state, within a week I was once again working in the fields out of fear that Angka would notice my absence. Now with rice harvesting time upon us, we were being coerced into working longer and harder. But the promise of more food being available still came too late for those people who were too weak to survive and literally hundreds of thousands of refugees died before our starvation came to an end. With the green fields now turning to gold and a good harvest at hand, we were instructed to plant our own individual gardens and that the food we grew would be our own. Once again, however, Angka deceived us by commandeering even this meager source of food. Although our conditions did temporarily improve marginally, we were soon placed on rations once again. Ultimately, anyone who used their so-called private garden as a personal food source would be executed. During this same period of time, the regime escalated its campaign against all people of non-Cambodian descent, in particular the Cambodian Chinese and the Vietnamese. When their constant efforts to uncover such people were successful, entire families were at risk of death. Summary executions by hitting the person in the back of the head with a heavy tool or by tying an individual's hands behind the back and placing the victim's head in plastic guaranteed a slow, barbaric death. One of my friends and her entire family lost their lives in this manner simply because Angka discovered that her mother could speak Vietnamese.

I was now eleven years old and I had already witnessed several lifetimes of unspeakable senseless inhumanity. There were no answers to the constant questions—why this cruelty toward innocent people, what was the purpose of this madness? Our only comfort in all of this was the support of loved ones. We were, at least, still together.

During this time, while I was still working in the girls' group we were once again assigned to another work site. The conditions were essentially the same as before except even more extreme. It was rice harvesting time which required us to remove the rice from the grain stalks. We did this from sunup to sometimes late at night working by moonlight. During the day, the heat was unbearable and many girls simply collapsed and lay where they had fallen. By now, I was completely bald and therefore with no hair to protect me from the constant sun. My feet were cracked from the hard ground which resulted in great pain every time I took another step. As if these circumstances were not brutal enough, now a new penalty was added to our working status. If an assigned job was not completed by sundown, we received no food that night. A second such failure resulted in the guilty party or parties being led away by guards not to be seen again. One way or another, it seemed like we were all destined to die in this work camp.

We worked for about two months under these conditions when, one morning, I noticed two strange women approaching us, paying particular attention to several of the young girls in my group. They were easy to identify as Angka guards because they were obviously well-fed and wore clean clothing, the black uniform of the regime.

I felt some degree of alarm at being the object of their attention and this struck terror in my heart. My worst fears were confirmed when I saw them approach our guards and engage them in conversation. They then walked towards the twelve of us and pointed to five girls including myself and ordered us to follow them to join the younger women's group, who were engaged in even harsher work conditions than we were. This meant leaving our families for even worse circumstances than I had experienced. I could not endure this news and my whole body started to tremble. These orders were to be followed immediately and we marched back into town to prepare for our departure.

I cannot recall my exact feelings; perhaps by now my senses were dulled. When I informed my mother of my new orders, her face drained of color and her eyes filled with tears. She reacted in a way that I knew would live with her for the rest of her life. This was too much for me and I started to scream for her as I was being led away. I was convinced now, that I had suffered the worst punishment that could have been given to me.

Almost in a state of paralysis I packed my possessions, which amounted to two pairs of pants, a second top and my treasured piece of black plastic and, through my tears, followed the two women out of Ksour as we started on our journey. My thoughts were filled with my family as I trudged on through the jungle. My father didn't even know that I was leaving, and I imagined the shock on his face when he would discover I was gone, perhaps forever. I was the youngest member of my seven brothers and sisters, all of us now, veterans of forced work camps and once again, facing an uncertain future. The only thing I knew for sure—if my new life was under the control of Angka, it would be brutal and maybe even fatal, but worse, I would now be completely alone.

The trip though the jungle and fields was long and difficult. We were a tragic and anxious group—young girls separated from family and friends forced into a life of even greater uncertainty than we had known. The laughter and derision of our guards crashed down on us like thunder. They were so strong and superior to us, knowing what the future held for us, we were mere sport for their game.

We arrived at our new camp late in the evening and were led to our new sleeping quarters. It was made of straw, and was about five feet in height, eight feet wide and 45 feet long. The only form of protection from the elements was a straw roof. This was to serve as my residence along with the other women for the immediate future.

That night, exhausted and frightened, I cried myself to sleep with my last thoughts of my mother and father and my family. I missed them so terribly, I thought my heart would break. Once again, I was left with the question of whether I would ever see them again, or even whether I would survive this new ominous ordeal. How many times can a person be victimized in this manner before she succumbs? I was completely alone again, far from my family and loved ones. My intuition of our treatment on this current march left me with a sense that even worse experiences were ahead of me. I was soon to discover how much I had already learned about my cruel captors and even more knowledge of them was to be gained from new insights.

For some reason at about this time I felt the need to communicate my feelings and began to write poetry, some of which I managed to save. From time-to-time, I would read the poems and thereby recreate a sense of attachment with my mother.[1]

We were aroused early the next morning by the sound of whistles—a sound that I had now come to associate with dread and loathing. There was no time to prepare ourselves. We were instantly marched off to the fields once again to use sickles for cutting rice and hay. I now discovered that this was the largest camp I had been in with literally thousands of other women, most older than I, with all of us bearing the unmistakable marks of suffering and privation in our faces and our bent posture.

Our work began before sunrise and the heat soon became intense. The women were arranged in a line, approximately six feet apart. We grabbed the hay in one hand and used our sickles to cut it with the other. In this fashion the entire row moved forward step-by-step, like so many automatons controlled by mechanical forces. I do not know how far the line stretched to my right and left, but as far as I could see there were women working in a bent position leaving nothing in their wake but bundles of hay. We worked continuously until noon despite the mounting heat and the increasing number of women who had collapsed and lay where they fell.

Our noon break lasted five minutes when we were given permission to get water from a nearby swamp. My back was in such pain I was unable to straighten up, and I walked to the swamp bent over in the same posture I was in when cutting hay. Our guards eyed us carefully while resting under the shade of the trees, drinking clean water and laughing while watching us slowly die. In what seemed the blink of an eye, the whistles blew again, signaling the order to those of us still standing to return to the fields. There was no further respite until the early evening, when we returned to the sleeping quarters. That evening, I knew my worst fears would be realized, when we were given even less food and water than before. If I had questioned my ability to survive my earlier experiences it seemed that all such questions were to be answered in my present circumstances.

Each day now was worse than the last one. Those of us who were lucky would catch a toad or lizard as we worked and quickly stuff it into our pocket to be eaten later. The work was back-breaking and the heat relentless. At night, spent with exhaustion and beyond any ordinary emotion I would lay on my small piece of black plastic, my thoughts with my family and reliving my happy childhood. During the rainy days when my sleeping quarters were under water, I would pile up sticks and brush to raise my bed of plastic above the water. Of course, this was only partially successful, and it seemed that I was constantly wet, either from rain or perspiration or both. Even in the evening, there was no relief from the constant badgering and bullying of Angka since this was the time they chose to remind us, over and over, that we weren't working hard enough and that those of us who didn't meet their ever-escalating standards would be appropriately dealt with.

UNFINISHED WORDS

Peaceful times have gone away
Long gone, so far, so far away

Let me live as I will you
Peaceful times as we once knew

The young, the old, so sad these days
So sad, so scared, are we

I have closed my eyes to run away
Run away to peaceful days

Mother please stay with me
Don't go, please stay close to me

I need you now to help me see
To see the days of peace for me

Help me find those peaceful times
The times we laughed when we were
free

No more pain, be at peace.

8

I had been at this camp living under these inhumane conditions for several weeks which, without saying, seemed like
an eternity. I had no contact with my family since the day I
was taken away and we were now informed that we would
shortly be moving to a new camp near the town of *Sras Koa*
even farther away. Numb with exhaustion, suffering from
chronic hunger, drained of all emotion, the thought of moving
even further from my family, struck me now as one further
step on a journey into oblivion.

The next day began like all the others over the last several
weeks except now we continued working after sundown and
well into the night since there was a full moon. During that
night, I learned that we would be responsible for building a
reservoir in Sras Koa and that the single men's group would
be working with us in this endeavor. For the first time in days,
I felt a spark of hope over the thought that my two brothers,
Thouch and Than, might be in that group.

The day before we were to depart for Sras Koa when we
marched out to the field, we saw the men's group already
assembled and working in the field. They were about 200 feet
from our group and as I continued to cut hay, I scanned the
group for familiar faces. Late that morning I thought I saw one

of my brothers in a crowd of men. I tried to signal by waving and calling discreetly while continuing to work so as not to draw the attention of the guards. I continued in this manner for some time, increasingly convinced that the man I saw was my third brother, Thouch. Finally, he noticed my signals and looked clearly in my direction. I was stunned when I realized that I was actually calling to my fourth brother, Than. It was an overwhelming, almost miraculous occurrence. I was so overjoyed to see him, I determined that we should not miss this opportunity to talk. I was so desperate for contact with my family that I would risk even discovery and possible death since it was forbidden for men and women to meet together.

During our five-minute break, I had noticed large piles of cut hay a short distance from where we were working and I signaled to him to make his way in that direction. Once he understood my meaning, he started moving in that direction while still engaged in a working posture. In a short while, we met behind a pile of hay which served to conceal us from the guards and I was so overcome with emotion that I started crying uncontrollably. He held me in his arms and when I had regained control, I quietly told him of my desperate circumstances and my only wish to rejoin the family. His face grew sad as he realized that we would now be sharing even more trying times. He urged me not to give up, and not to let Angka end my life. We stayed together as long as we could and then broke away with sad hearts as we made our way back to our respective groups.

Later, to add to my despair, I felt guilty that I had unburdened my feelings on my brother in this manner. He was suffering no less than I was and I should not have added my hardship to his.

That night again was a time for reflection and an attempt to answer the question of why? Why so many deaths, why such cruel treatment, how many more would needlessly die at the hands of our barbaric captors, and finally, would my family survive?

The next morning came very quickly. We were all rushed to an assembly and informed that we would be leaving for our new assignment immediately. Once again, I was left with the same unanswered questions I had raised in my mind so often. As we started on the road to our new camp, I looked back at the horrible camp and the brutal rice fields that had claimed so many lives. Was there any reason to believe that life would be any different in the new camp?

We had walked for about three hours in heat so intense that many of us struggled to keep up. My feet once again swelled up and blistered bringing pain with every step. At about one o'clock we were told that we would soon be at the new camp. Shortly thereafter, we emerged out of the brush and approached an abandoned freeway littered with wrecked and disabled vehicles on the roadsides. This was the first example of a paved road that I had seen in two years. As we were marched down the freeway, I searched for grass to walk on which eased the pain in my feet.

After walking a short distance we were led off the freeway and marched down the side of a hill. As we descended, Angka announced that our new camp was close at hand and that our assignment was to build a reservoir on this site. Finally, we were led to a large clearing where even the earth looked tortured, so barren and dry that it was much like a desert. This terrible landscape was to be the site of our new camp for as long as it would take to complete our next assignment.

Our first task was to gather wood and brush in order to pre-pare our sleeping quarters. I now had considerable experience in this task and even though I was younger than the other women in my group I worked as hard as I could to keep up.

That night, I wondered at the impossibility of digging a reservoir in such a desolate location. Even as an eleven year old, I realized that the ground was too hard and dry for such a purpose. This assignment would again result in a great num-ber of deaths and that perhaps this was the real reason for our being brought here. Once again, my worst premonition was to be confirmed.

The next morning, we marched about a quarter of a mile from the camp, given sticks to dig with and, after warning us not to complain or talk, we began the task of digging the reservoir. Given the extreme heat and the difficult labor, in a short time, all of us were exhausted. To add to my own diffi-culties, my feet continued to swell, and I walked in great pain as we carried the dirt away from the site of the digging.

When we were finally allowed to stop to eat at noon, I noticed the arrival of great numbers of women. It soon became very crowded at the work-site and I wondered if the single men's group would also join us in hopes that I would see my brother again. We were told that the reservoir would be more than two kilometers square, 20 meters on the bottom, four meters above the ground level, and ten meters across the top. Moreover, this was to be entirely dug and erected by hand and to be completed in about ten months. Perhaps the high mortality rate to be expected, explained why so many people were involved in the project.

The first day of this assignment introduced me to a new dimension in Angka brutality that I had never imagined, even in my worst times. Aside from the degree of physical effort involved in continuously carrying heavy loads of dirt by hand, the length of our work day was extended beyond the usual evening schedule. Within two weeks, we were being aroused at 3:00 a.m. and our work started immediately thereafter. We were now working about 18 hours a day under a hot sun which further sapped what little energy we had left for our labors. Angka watched relentlessly in shade and comfort, all the while making sport of us and laughing at those who fell, too weak or sick to continue. My resolve to maintain as emotionally detached as possible was tested on many occasions. It would have been so easy to give in to my hatred of these cruel people in their black shirts who laughed as we cried.

Each day, we were joined by large numbers of women to replace those who had died of exhaustion, sickness or were killed by the guards. Those of us who carried on were constantly covered by dirt with our clothing nothing but rags and tatters. If one fell ill with fever, a common occurrence under such conditions, begging off from work only resulted in greater abuse. There was no relief from the cruelty of our tormentors and no circumstance too extreme to allow for any reason not to work. On those occasions when I was sick with fever and had to struggle simply to breathe, I chose to work rather than give the guards a reason to chastise and threaten me. Once, in late March or early April, I was carrying the dirt up to the top of the reservoir whose walls had now been shaped into a steep incline. The heat and my weakened condition caused me to become dizzy, and I staggered under the weight of the load. My feet gave way, and I collapsed falling to the bottom of the hole. If it had been filled with water, I would surely have drowned. As it was, I lost consciousness for a few moments. When I regained my senses, the Black Shirts were standing over me. They dragged me to a shaded area and told me that I had ten minutes to rest and then I must return to work. It wasn't necessary for them to tell me what would happen if I failed to comply. I do not know to this day how I managed to go on, but somehow, I roused myself and returned to work under the hostile gaze of the guards who watched me carefully to see if I should falter once again. When I finally got to my sleeping place that evening I thought that I had achieved some small victory in that Angka would not end my life that day.

The months slowly passed in this tortured manner with no reason to believe that my life would change in any significant way. Perhaps I was fated to spend whatever days were left of my short life in this manner, forever climbing the wall of the reservoir, emptying dirt on the top, and then returning to the bottom in an endless fashion. Each night I would fall exhausted on my black plastic, crying myself to sleep while thinking of my family and wondering if we would ever be together again.

Soon the rainy season came and, although the climate was cooler, we simply traded the heat of the sun for the constant dampness. Now we ate, worked and slept in the rain, often half submerged in mud. Sometimes, the rain was so heavy we literally slept under water, too tired to move.

Even worse, the ground turned into a quagmire and climbing the hill now became even more torturous than before, since the footing was totally insecure. To add to our plight, the rain also caused snakes and scorpions to seek new ground and many people were being bitten especially as they slept. In fact, the rate of deaths from various causes including suicide continued to increase at an alarming rate.

Despite our hardship, there were occasional experiences of a more positive nature. There were varying degrees of friendship and support that emerged among the women. Although most of us regarded alliances with suspicion for fear of accusations by an Angka confidante, still the need for social contact was so great that we often threw caution to the wind and with some hesitation would attempt as normal a friendship as possible under the circumstances. Needless to say, Angka attempted to discourage any attempts at friendly relationships. They were particularly suspicious of older women expressing any gesture of friendliness toward a younger woman. If this persisted, such women were often executed, so extreme was their concern in this area.

But there were less overt examples of cooperation which could not be repressed. Some women made hats out of palm leaves which offered at least some protection from the elements. My initial efforts at hat-making were not very successful and brought good-natured laughter from the other women. However, I continued to watch the process carefully and my second effort was much more successful.

During this time we would also be subjected to random checks by Angka, a practice that was greeted with secret laughter. None of us had anything of value besides the poor clothing that we wore, since everything of worth had been confiscated long ago. This simply made me realize that not only were our guards cruel and uneducated but they were also stupid.

As July approached our living conditions deteriorated even further. Just as before, our food rations continued to decline until we were now existing on about one-third of the already reduced diet and anything we could find in the fields. I often resorted to chewing on wild chestnut roots and leaves, since this temporarily eased the hunger pains. If I was particularly fortunate, I might find some wild berries or potatoes. One had to be especially careful however, since much of the vegetation was poisonous, and I watched many people become sick and die after eating something toxic out of sheer desperation. Once again, disease spread rapidly throughout the camp resulting in more fatalities. I often wondered how I managed to survive such conditions and I thought that it was my youth that was responsible, since the largest number of deaths were among the older women. This observation, in turn, increased my concern for my mother's welfare.

As our circumstances worsened, more and more women attempted to escape the camp. Almost all were caught and then forced to work under even harsher conditions resulting in a slow, painful death, an object lesson for those of us who still survived. To reinforce their message, Angka now required us to attend meetings at night where they warned us of the risks of escape. All this accomplished, however, was to deprive us of much needed sleep. I had now been in this camp about six months. Although we heard constant rumors that the men's group was on the other side of the reservoir, we had not actually seen them. I hoped with all my heart that my brothers were still alive and part of that group. If so, I should see them soon.

In the meantime, our work on the reservoir continued. At our evening meetings, we were exhorted to work harder and faster since once our task was completed, the work assignments would be reduced, or so we were told. I doubt that anyone believed these stories; I certainly did not, having heard Angka lies for well over two years. As I looked around at the faces of the other women at these meetings, all I saw was despair, exhaustion and starvation. These feeble attempts to instill hope were certainly not going to convince those of the group who were close to death. My one consolation was that as the wall of the reservoir continued to rise, my brothers would be on the other side and that we were getting closer to one another with each bucket of dirt. Although I was now convinced that I would not survive much longer, I wanted to see them one more time and to tell them how much I loved them and the others members of my family before I died. Perhaps, then, they, in turn, would relate my last dying thoughts to my parents.

By now, the reservoir was about three-fourths completed, and the daily walk to what was to be the top of the work site was about a mile. Since this was regarded by our captors as an inefficient way to use our time, we were ordered to move our sleeping quarters closer to the walls. The next day we moved the camp to the new site which we found to be infested with mosquitos and other insects which caused much consternation among the women. For my part, I tried to ignore this new torture by focussing on the fact that this move brought me closer to the men's group.

That night, Angka informed us that we would be attending a meeting and that all of the men and women working on this project were to be present. My heart leaped with joy at the news that I might finally see my brothers.

The meeting was held in a large open field that was to hold the thousands of people who were working on the reservoir. The sight of the large numbers involved in the construction disheartened me with the growing realization that, even if my brothers were part of this project, it would be a miracle for us to find one another in this multitude.

As the crowd began to join at the field site, we heard music playing. The theme, of course, centered on the "joys" of work and how happy we should be that we were close to completing such an enormous undertaking. There was no mention, of course, of the countless number of lives that had been lost in the outcome. Since I had not heard any music from the time we were forced out of my home in Phnom Penh in 1975, I was struck by how different these sounds were from the music I heard as a child.

Finally, after the entire crowd had gathered, the music stopped and the leader of the Angka group started to address us. His message was predictable enough. A promise that when the reservoir was completed we would be allowed to return to our families and that our lives would be improved, and so forth. For one brief moment my spirit soared at the news but then, even at my age, I understood the caliber of the people who were making these promises. His harangue continued for hours and, since I had started working at 3 a.m. the previous morning, I found it increasingly more difficult to keep my eyes open. Each time I fell asleep, the lady next to me would shake me awake, since being seen asleep at these meetings would result in beatings or worse.

The mass meeting lasted until well into the morning and when we were aroused to begin working, we had only two hours of sleep. Despite our fatigue an atmosphere of optimism swept across the camp. Perhaps it was in part due to the project's impending completion, perhaps some of us allowed some hope that the leader's promises would this time be realized, perhaps it was the result of having seen or believing that family and friends were nearby or some combination of these factors. In any event, we set forth to complete the job with particular vigor. There were thousands of us, working with the same dream, with the hope of leaving this God-forsaken site, and returning to our loved ones.

The next day, we found ourselves working close to one of the men's groups. As difficult as our conditions were, the men were actually being forced to run up the side of the reservoir with their load of dirt. As I continued to work, I moved gradually closer to the men, being cautious not to arouse suspicion since it was forbidden for members of one group to make contact with the members of another group. As the day passed, and I continued my secret search for a family member, I noticed a man working about a hundred feet away from me who looked familiar to me. I slowly worked my way in his direction, gradually narrowing the distance between us. When I was within about 20 feet away, I stood erect and as casually as I could glanced sharply in his direction. My heart skipped a beat as I recognized the face of my fourth brother, Than. He hadn't yet seen me, and I immediately started to calculate a safe way to make my presence known.

It was now late morning and we would soon be taking the customary brief break, and I was determined to use the opportunity for our contact. I was now within ten feet of him and signalled with a series of gestures to draw his attention. Finally, I caught his eye and he turned his head and saw me. I saw the shock of recognition on his face and then he allowed a small smile at the knowledge that I was still alive and now so close. When he understood my purpose, he slowly moved closer to me and when the whistles blew for our brief rest, we sat down close enough to hold a quiet conversation. I bowed my head and began to speak in a low tone of voice, trying not to move my lips or give any sign that we were actually conversing. Remembering the last time when I met Than under similar circumstances, I tried to maintain some measure of control by asking about his health and that of my other family members. He answered me that he was fine and that my other brother, Thouch, was also alive and well. His next words expressed his concern for me, that he couldn't believe I had survived this camp and that I now must resolve myself to stay safe and be careful. This was too much for me. His total disregard for his own welfare and his only concern for mine brought tears to my eyes, and I was overcome with emotion. Nevertheless, I knew instinctively that I could not allow myself to continue in this fashion for both our safety.

I forced myself to regain my composure and when I looked up, I noticed immediately that two guards from the men's group were looking in my direction. My brother sensed my alarm and slowly stood up and walked way. Shortly thereafter the whistles blew again signaling our return to work. There was no more time to contemplate this meeting. Any further unusual behavior on my part would certainly have aroused additional suspicion, and I attempted to continue working throughout the rest of the day with no outward sign of any change in my circumstances.

Later, in my sleeping quarters, I allowed myself a secret moment of pleasure. At least three of us were still alive. But we had been away from our family for over a year and, if they were still alive, surely they must be worried about us.

During the next week there was no opportunity to meet with my brother again. But now, the reservoir was almost completed and Angka celebrated the occasion by giving us cigarettes. I thought immediately how wonderful it would be if I could get them to my brother.

The only simple way to do this would be to sneak out of our camp right after the mid-day meal and make our way into the men's camp, but such an offense would involve a terrible risk if we were caught. Nevertheless, the urge to see my brother and to offer some small gift was so great I decided to take the chance. I approached another girl who I knew also had a brother in the men's camp and, throwing caution to the winds since she could easily have reported me to the guards, asked her to join me. Much to my relief she agreed to my foolish plan. The next day, after we had eaten our lunch, we quietly left the camp and stole our way in the direction of the men's camp which was about 20 minutes away through heavy underbrush. We made our way through the thicket as quickly as we could. Suddenly we came upon a man who was working in the forest and without giving it any thought we approached him and simply explained our mission. After recovering from his shock and glancing around to see if we were being observed he admonished us for our stupid behavior. Nevertheless, he told us to wait where we were and that he would send our two brothers to meet us. As we waited, our knees started to tremble and our hearts were beating loud enough to be heard by others. What if this was a trap and he would return with Angka guards? They would surely execute us on the spot.

After what seemed like an eternity, we heard the sound of steps approaching and my friend and I almost died of fright until we recognized our two brothers emerge from the trees and approach us. We were so overcome with relief and joy, we rushed to them and embraced them. After our short greeting they told us we had been foolish to do this and that we must return immediately.

Just as we turned back to our camp, the head of the men's group stepped out from behind a tree and ordered us to stop. He then turned to my brother, Than, and asked who we were. Now, as our terror began to escalate, Than started to plead with the man by explaining that we were their sisters and had simply wanted to meet for just a few minutes. The man walked closer to us and recognized that we were two terribly frightened children. He then instructed our brothers to return to their camp and then he turned back to us with a look of such intense anger, I experienced the greatest terror of my life.

He directed us to sit on the ground with our backs to one another and, when we had complied, he tied our arms and hands together and told us that he was going to take us back to the men's camp and that we would be dealt with there.

We both began to cry, and I pleaded with him to show us mercy or, if he was going to kill us to do it here and to do it quickly so we would not have to suffer. But my pleas fell on deaf ears, and I knew that our lives were at an end when he told us that we had violated the rules and he would make an example of us.

He forced us to our feet and, bound like animals, he marched us back to the men's camp. Everyone came out of their resting quarters to stare at these two young girls who had obviously committed some serious offense. My brother, of course, reacted to our circumstances with an expression of horror and yet I knew he was as helpless in this situation as I was. I knew he was thinking that our capture was his fault, and I wanted to cry out to him that he was not to blame for my mistake.

The guards from the men's group marched us through the
camp as if we were some prize for all to see. I will never forget their arrogance and contempt as long as I live.

Within a short time two of the women guards from our
group arrived in the men's camp and, after some discussion
with the men's guards, they informed us that they were taking
us back to the women's group where we would be appropriately dealt with. The march back to the women's camp was
another nightmare. Bound and frightened beyond belief, we
could only imagine what would happen to us on our return.
When we arrived back at the women's camp, we were told to
sit down and to wait for our punishment. Once again, we
were left with our private thoughts to contemplate our fate. I
had seen many of my country people summarily executed,
some in horrible ways for lesser crimes than what we had
committed. It was no stretch of the imagination to convince
myself that my life was over.

After about 30 minutes of this mental torture, our guard
returned and told us how we would be punished. Our food
rations were to be reduced by half for one week and we were
to be made an example of in front of the rest of the women.
The only reason we were to be spared from an even worse
fate and certain death we were told was our youth.

Over the next week while our punishment was being exacted, I wondered many times if a quick and certain death might
have been preferable. As the lack of food took its toll, I
became increasingly weak and unable to stand without experiencing dizziness. My desperate condition was now obvious
to everyone and served as a constant reminder to others of the
consequences of my crime. The guards continued to humiliate me at every opportunity, prodding me, announcing to one

and all that this is what happens to people who break the rules.

Once again, I resolved to hide my emotions, not to let them know that I was weak and in pain. But now I burned with as much fierce anger inside as a 12-year old could muster. My hatred for these cruel, barbarous people became an all encompassing emotion. I vowed that one day, if possible, I would do whatever I could to inform the civilized world of the suffering and death inflicted by Angka on innocent people.

I cannot offer any explanation but somehow I survived the week of punishment that my captors inflicted on me. I began to think that perhaps I would now live through almost any treatment that they might impose. During that week, construction of the reservoir was in its final stages and we had been told once again that our return to our families was imminent, and I know that this hope, no matter how remote, sustained me during that week of torment.

One day after work we were told that a meeting was to be held that night involving all the women working on the project. This announcement was met with great anticipation since we thought that we would finally learn that our return to our families had been officially decided. Once again, however, we realized the deceit of our captors. The crushing news came at us like a hammer blow. Not only were we told that returning to our families was out of the question, but rather, we were to be moved again to another work site near the reservoir to clear the land and plant more rice.

By now, after so many similar disappointments and lies, we simply reacted without emotion and quietly accepted the news in a submissive manner. What choice did we have?

We started on our new journey early the next morning.

There were about 250 young women in the group, many of whom had replaced those who had died earlier. A cold front had moved into the area overnight bringing with it a hard rain which turned the earth into mud. A fitting and proper circumstance to match our state of mind.

We marched the entire day in the rain. As the temperature continued to drop, our bodies became chilled, making each step a nightmare. Finally, we stopped at an old, large deserted barn with only half a roof for shelter. I spent that night in the mud inside the barn, lying in a row with all of the others and only my small piece of black plastic to separate my body from the cold and the rain.

The next morning we were led to the rice field and forced to work in water up to our knees. The sky was thick with dark clouds and the water chilled us to our bones. It was the same every day. Heavy gloomy clouds and constant rain. At midday, we stopped to eat our first meal at this camp. The food was the same, rice and water, meager rations which would not long prevent us dying in the cold water, far from our families.

During our brief rest, I placed my plastic against the wall of the barn and listened to the rain now driving hard against the mold-covered wood above my head. How strange, I thought, that the same rain that was always welcome in my younger years would now add to my torment. My sadness was too overwhelming, and I began to cry. There was no time for even a small measure of reminiscing, however, as the hated whistles once again signalled the time to return to the fields. We slowly marched back to our area and continued working. Here again, we discovered that there were leaches in the field, only now, we accepted this as simply another condition of our miserable existence. Many of the women were no longer alarmed by them or even attempted to remove them, so fatigued were they. However, I was still terrified by them and begged my fellow workers to remove them from my body whenever I discovered one.

The next day, as we marched back into the fields in a freezing rain, I began to feel feverish and dizzy. My legs collapsed under me, and I fell into the mud. I struggled desperately to regain my balance, but each time I stood up, I would fall again. I became aware that my erratic behavior was being noticed by our guard who shouted at me that I must keep up with the rest of the work force. I was at a point, however, that I no longer cared for the reactions of my captors. I was so weak, my body so fragile, and my emotional state so desperate that the actions of Angka were no longer of any consequence to me.

I managed to continue working throughout the day and finally we were allowed to return to our sleeping quarters. I was so feverish that I became semi-comatose. Now, I was more convinced that I was near death than at any time in the past and I prepared myself to accept this fact. Over the next several weeks as I lay huddled on the floor of the barn, I heard my mother's voice urging me to remain strong and that I must help myself if I was to recover. She reminded me that there were many wild plants that could be used to counter the fever.

Somehow, I roused myself from my weakened condition and I stole out of the camp in search of anything growing in the wild that might help. I repeated this same practice over the next several nights and, miraculously, the fever began to subside. By the fourth day my strength returned and that night I thanked God for my recovery and for the continued hope that I still might live to see my mother and father.

During this time, I learned once again how near at hand death was to all of us. My only close friend, Chee, who had shared many experiences with me including stealing into the men's camp to visit our brothers, tried to help me through my illness. She was a great comfort to me in this time of need. Then, about a week after I recovered word came to us that her mother had died. We, of course, didn't know the circumstances of her death but she was devastated and completely depressed by the news, as I would have been.

Although I tried as best I could to comfort her, her grief was overwhelming and she could do no more than repeat over and over that she too wished to die. It was a scene I had witnessed too many times, and I could only hope that time would help her recover from her terrible loss.

We were, by now, close to completing our work assignment and we were told once again that we would soon be back with our families. I could not conceal my mistrust of these people and so I did not share in the enthusiasm of the other women. Nevertheless, as the days passed and the promises were repeated, even I began to believe that this time, Angka would actually reunite us again. Still, I held back for fear of being duped once more. However, we woke one morning and were instructed to break camp—we were to return to Ksour which we had left almost fifteen months ago to see our loved ones again. Were they alive?

The trip back involved a long march over a considerable distance, but we all found renewed strength as every step brought us closer to family and friends. But now, this hope was coupled with a number of growing concerns. It had been almost two years since I had seen or heard of my mother and my other family members. What if they were not alive? What if they had moved? Would they recognize me, now a girl of twelve who had changed in so many ways?

Finally, we neared the outskirts of the town I had been taken from, for what seemed like an eternity ago. My heart was pounding in my chest with each step and I was almost unable to restrain myself from running to my mother's hut. But we were required to march together as a group, without talking and to maintain discipline. It was now growing dark, and we stopped at an old dilapidated temple where we were instructed to bed down for the night wherever we could since this was to be our new camp site. But the thought of being so close to my mother and having to wait at least another day to see her was simply more than I could bear. I pleaded with the guard to let me search for my family that night and that I would do extra work if she consented. Perhaps sensing my desperation, and in what was the only example of sympathy I ever witnessed from Angka, to my great relief she consented to my request. Before she could change her mind, I quickly turned and started to walk down the main path of the village in the direction of my mother's hut.

As I walked down the dark deserted path using the moonlight as my guide, even though my release from my captors was temporary, I realized a fuller awareness of my surroundings than I had in a long time. I heard the sound of the crickets and I felt the presence of the wind against my body. These were sensations that brought a measure of serenity as I approached the hut that was our family's temporary home. I paused for a moment before entering, my heart pounding in my chest, just to make sure that this was not one of my many dreams. I entered through the doorway and stopped, looking and hoping that my mother would appear. At that very instant, she and my sister, Chan, emerged from inside the house and they stopped short as if they couldn't believe their eyes. Then we rushed to one another trembling with joy and crying as we had never done so before, our emotions flooding over us. The feeling of being held in my mother's embrace after almost two years of separation and not knowing if I would ever see her again was so intense that it left me breathless. We clutched each other as if to say we would never be separated again, my head buried in her embrace, her tears mixing with mine.

Slowly we began to recover from our emotional state and my mother and sister began to study my condition in more detail. My fragile status was my mother's next concern and she began to search for food. We talked through the night, describing our experiences and by silent, mutual consent trying to minimize the horrors that we had all witnessed during that time. I wanted to tell her that it was her love that sustained me through the painful times, especially on those occasions when I thought my death was imminent. But my feelings were so complicated and I knew that she was still enduring much distress over the uncertainty of the other members of our family that I thought this would only add to her burden.

When I asked about my father's whereabouts a look of concern again came over her face and she told me that she heard recently that he was still working in the jungle with the men's group. Even though the news was reassuring, it was evident that she was quietly suffering from their separation. I also learned that my fifth brother, Thoeun, who was the youngest of the males in my family, had been taken away five months ago. Even though by now an underground communication network had been formulated, she had heard nothing about his whereabouts because no one had received any news of his group.

Angka's plan of separating families especially husbands from wives and youngest children from their parents, had served to scatter all of my loved ones throughout the country. This, of course, served their purpose of reducing resistance and forcing us to be totally dependent on them for our survival. They believed that any loyalty to our families would be so disrupted by these experiences that they would then govern a nation of submissive individuals who would no longer question their authority.

They failed to take into account, however, the strength of family ties in their strategy, which proved, in the long run, to overcome their efforts. In my own case, my experiences only increased my hatred of Angka and my resolve to be reunited with my family. No matter how terrible their threats, my love for my mother and father and my siblings would never change.

As we talked through the night I learned that although there had been many men living in this town at first, they had been gradually led off by Angka during the night never to return and now only a few were left. In some cases, public executions were also conducted. I learned for the first time of the death of my sister-in-law Savvy's, 19-year old brother, Haing, the second of her siblings to die at the hands of Angka. Driven by hunger, he had stolen a tiny fish from an Angka storehouse. He was, however, caught in the act and, with hands tied behind his back, dragged to the center of the town where he was literally beaten to death by Angka guards. This incident was related to me by my mother who had witnessed his torture and eventual death. Of all the brutalities she had seen and experienced, this was perhaps the one incident that had the most profound impact on her – one which she would remember forever.

The disappearance of the men was a matter of much speculation among the women of Ksour, but my mother was convinced that this circumstance was, again, an effort by Angka to maintain control over our lives since the news of the death camps had started to filter back to the town and the men in Ksour were becoming increasingly frightened. I fell asleep that night close to my mother for the first time in almost two years, once again simply as a child whose only wish was to be safe and secure.

The next morning, I had to face the hated prospect of having to return to my group for our next work assignment. At least this time, however, my mother would be nearby and this made my departure a little easier.

It was still dark when I started out to my camp site. My mother had given me a piece of sweet potato that she had found, and I held it in my hand as I walked through the jungle, as the one tangible sign of my recent reunion with my mother and sister. When I rejoined my group, it was easy to see from the expression on the faces of the other girls which ones had received good news of their families' circumstances and which ones had learned that family members were gone, dead, or missing.

When we met with our group leaders that morning we were told that we would be working in the rice fields a short distance from the camp which meant that I would be close to my mother and my sister in Ksour. This heartening news was also followed by the announcement, however, that this assignment was to be only of short duration. When the planting was completed we would be moved to another campsite far away whose destination was unknown.

The news that we would be starting a new cycle of moving and planting left me with a feeling of deep despair. After the brief reunion with my mother and sister and the renewed hope that the nightmare of the last two years might be over, I was once again faced with an uncertain future and the possibility of never seeing my family again. I had seen more tragedy and devastation in my young life than most adults encounter in many lifetimes. The almost constant privation and despair interrupted by brief moments of happiness had taken its emotional toll. Still, I had also learned much in the last two years especially about my captors and the regime that they stood for. Often their practices drove us to an emotional brink because of their contradictory nature. A case in point occurred when some of the workers would be involved in boiling palm syrup in a huge pot to distill the sugar content. This task usually was completed at noon time, coinciding with our brief break for lunch. The rich, sweet smell of the sugar drove us to distraction and longing for some small taste. We would gather around the pot with great anticipation hoping that some of the hard brown particles would be left after the syrup had been removed. For some reason, our desperate behavior which was the direct outcome of their systematic starvation efforts, embarrassed Angka. They would then drive us away with threats that our rations would be further reduced if our ingratitude continued.

Yet in the face of all the hardship and brutality that my people had endured, there was still, for most of us, the belief that some day this would end; that despite all the evidence to the contrary, Angka would change rather than continue on the road to total destruction. Increasingly, however, I came to the inescapable conclusion that the brutality would not end of its own initiative. We had learned that the leader of Angka, a man named Pol Pot, was bent on restructuring Cambodia, regardless of the cost in human lives and suffering. There may have been other tyrants in the history of the human race but no one who was more despised and reviled by his own people than this madman who had embarked on mass annihilation and slavery. Once we were an enterprising people, hard working, committed to our strong family heritage, with each successive generation striving to improve the lives of everyone. Now, our spirits were broken, our hopes and dreams destroyed, living a sub-human existence in terror, sorrow and confusion. The hundreds and hundreds of dead lying in the streets and the fields where they fell, the tears of mother's crying over the bodies of their loved ones were such common sights that it seemed like our country would never again achieve a measure of peace and serenity. It was November of 1977, the depths of my country's despair. We were to learn that by now, about two million of the pre-Angka population of our seven million people or about a third had died as a direct result of Angka practices. It seemed that the strength of Angka was increasing every day while the bodies of my country people mounted.

I continued my present assignment for another two weeks, in close proximity to my mother and sister. My concern for their welfare continued to increase since Angka considered that anyone who lived in town to be essentially expendable and they were constantly reminded of their worthlessness and inability to contribute to the restructuring plan by virtue of their age, illness, or other circumstances. In most respects, perhaps their lives were as horrible as those of us assigned to the death camps since their level of subsistence was even poorer than ours.

The next day, the news came that we were to be moved. Much to my surprise the march to our new campsite was only about three miles, still a relatively short distance from my mother in Ksour. The camp site was a thin stretch of flat land perhaps 10 meters long surrounded by deep water on one side and rice fields on the other, much like a peninsula in shape. By now, the routine was a familiar one. We each set out to build our camp and the next morning the back breaking work of long hours in the rice fields began again. It was as if the brief respite from trudging in the water and mud had been just a dream. Once again, continuous hunger and exhaustion were to be the reality.

The first night in the new work camp I was surprised to find that our food ration was more than we usually received and amounted to about one handful of rice. Even though this was still less than we needed, I was determined to share some of it with my mother and sister. After I finished about half of the rice soup, I placed the remainder in a metal container and I approached my friend, Chee, and told her of my plans, hoping that she would join me. Her first reaction was to refuse, remembering what happened on our last such endeavor. But when she saw how determined I was, she agreed to accompany me.

We waited for total darkness and the quiet that signaled everyone was asleep. At the right moment, we crawled out of the camp and made our way through the rice paddies into the jungle. By now we were both accomplished at traveling under such conditions and moved swiftly through the jungle growth.

At one point, we heard wild dogs barking close by apparently searching for food in the jungle, but fortunately, we didn't encounter them. Now, however, we came across a large body of water which ran between the campsite and the town. The thought of having to cross to the other side was terrifying—we had no way of knowing how deep and cold it might be and neither of us had learned to swim. We waded in searching for a place to cross that might be safe. At some places the water reached to our chins, but as we continued downstream we suddenly saw the glimmer of lights from the huts of Ksour through the dark and we crossed over with great relief. When we stepped on shore, we moved as quickly as we could to our respective huts. I found my mother and sister as before and, ignoring their expressions of surprise and concern, I handed them the rice. I told my mother that I was so worried about her it was impossible for me to eat the whole meal without sharing some of it with her. By now, they were both overcome with emotion and we hugged one another through our tears. She held me tight and told me that I must never take such a risk again, that she and my sister would be all right. From now on, she said, I must eat all of my food to stay strong and as the youngest member of the family, it was my responsibility to survive.

Later that night, my sister and I spoke in private. She admitted that the people of the town were living under desperate circumstances. I knew this to be true first hand from their appearance and the look of hunger and despair in the faces of all the townspeople. The worst agony for me was that there wasn't anything I could say or do that might help. My sister, Chan, was doing everything humanly possible for my mother and my niece, Karin, which was to help them survive in the midst of their brutal physical and emotional existence. The irony of this situation was that Chan was considered to be worthless in the eyes of Angka because of a crippling lower leg infection that severely impaired her ability to walk. Yet this same condition served our purpose of providing our mother with someone who could help her through this nightmare.

I left them with a sad heart, remembering the tearful expression on their faces as I joined up with my friend, Chee, and made our way back to our camp. We returned to our sleeping quarters without causing any alarm. As we laid down, our relief at not being discovered mixed with our despair over the conditions in the town. Before we fell asleep we whispered our reassurances to one another. We knew that we had taken a great risk but that it needed to be done.

The next day started as all the others before. Back-breaking brutal field work which quickly sapped all of our strength. Still my thoughts were with my mother and sister and their desperate condition. I began to collect the tiny crabs that lived in the rice paddies and placed them in the pocket of my blouse. They would provide some degree of nourishment for my mother, Chan, and my niece later that evening. At noon, however, when we gathered for our portion of rice soup, our guards made everyone empty their pockets and confiscated the crabs. Once again, a small reminder of their senseless cruelty.

Later that day, while working in the fields, I overheard one of our guards tell another that we would need more women because of the size of the field. I was terrified by this news since this meant that my sister, Chan, might be among those who would be forced to join the work group. I immediately recognized the double risk involved: my mother would now be left completely alone and forced to survive on her own, and my sister might not survive the physical strain of field work in her already weak condition. I started to make plans to leave the camp that night in order to get word to my mother and sister of the impending plans but when we returned to our sleeping quarters that evening, I realized that it was too late. A large group of women and young girls had already arrived from the town and were receiving instructions for field work.

As I searched through the newcomers to see if my sister was one of them, I realized how I must have reacted almost two years ago under similar circumstances. The women were all huddled together, terror stricken at this new nightmare that had been visited on them by Angka. I walked through each cluster, trying to offer them some reassurance and hoping desperately that somehow, my sister was still among those in the town, and then I spotted Chan standing in the middle of about 20 young women, thin as a reed with a terrified expression on her face. I wanted to go to her and throw my arms around her and to offer whatever comfort I could, but I knew this would have to wait.

I watched from a distance and heard the guard order her group to join ours. I was right to refrain from approaching her earlier since they would not have allowed this if they knew we were sisters. Chan, of course, did not know that she would be joining me and I waited until she and the other women with her made their way to our sleeping area. I quietly approached and, signaling her to say nothing but to remain silent, I whispered to her that I would explain my actions to her when it was safe. Later, after everyone was asleep, I made my way to her and, as briefly as I could, shared some of the rules for survival in the work camp.

9

Over the next three weeks I tried as best as I could to help Chan adjust to our harsh lifestyle without arousing suspicion. It broke my heart to see my sister undergoing the same experiences I had at first. The day came when we were finally confronted by one of the guards who asked if we were sisters. I responded quickly that we were just friends and when the guard walked away, apparently convinced of my explanation, I repeated my prior instructions to her and asked that she must be very careful in what she said to the other women. I also shared the news with her that I had heard of the possibility that we might be moving soon and this might mean our going to different camps.

Almost from the day that my sister came to the camp she and I had secretly planned to visit our mother at least one more time before we were to be moved to the new camp. Since this was now imminent, together with my friend, Chee, the three of us slipped out of camp and made our way through the jungle to my mother's hut.

Even though we moved in silence, I could sense my sister's fear, a reminder of my own reactions the first time I had stolen out of camp at night. When we came to the body of water, my sister drew back and would not enter it. The sound of the

wild dogs barking nearby made the experience even more terrifying for her. After much reassurance, Chee and I each took
her hand and led her safely across to the town side of the river.
We moved swiftly through the town and down the now familiar path to our mother's hut. We quietly called out to her, and
she appeared at the entrance, her fright and despair changing
quickly to joy at the sight of her two youngest daughters. As
before, we shared what we could of our food ration and it did
our hearts good to know that this little bit of nourishment
would sustain her further. Now, since she was living just with
my niece, we also brought a bucket of water for them, since
she was unable to do this for herself.

That night as we lay together in what might be our last night
before we were to be separated again, I wrestled with the
questions that were uppermost in mind. Where would my
mother get food? What would happen to her if she got sick?
My body shook as I thought of her being alone now, with no
family members to care for her. In her sleep, my mother felt
my body shaking and reached out to comfort me. We both
lay there silently, each of us more concerned for the other's
welfare than for our own.

We left before sunup in order to return before our absence
was discovered. As we made our way back through the jungle, I could tell from the expression on my sister's face that she
was experiencing the same degree of emotional strain that I
was. We tried to hide our tears from one another, but of course
we each knew that our mother's health was uppermost in our
minds.

The work in the rice fields continued to become more difficult while our food rations decreased. This assignment was
again, a repetition of all of my previous experiences. At least

this time, I had my sister as a companion and we tried as best we could to care for one another, sharing food, sharing our sleeping area, sharing our feelings just to get through each day. A month passed in this manner and then the dreaded announcement was made at a camp meeting that we would shortly be moving again. Of course, there was no way of knowing when we would go, how long we would be gone, whether my sister would be in the same group. But the most important question for both of us was would we be able to visit with our mother. Then one morning we were told to gather our possessions to move to the new work site. There was no time to get a message to my mother. We simply collected in the center of the camp and were led down the road to our new destination. We marched throughout the day down a dry, abandoned rice field. As we continued our march, we saw nothing that would suggest human habitation, only open fields with weeds as tall as I was. The dust blew across the landscape with no trees or growth to hinder its movement. If there ever had been people in this barren land, they had left it a long time ago.

Finally, late that afternoon we reached our new campsite. I had hoped there would be some trees or vegetation, but what we saw as far as our eyes could see was a hot, dry abandoned, desperate landscape, a suitable metaphor for our own condition. I knew instantly that to remain here for any time was certain death sentence.

We were again instructed to set up our camp. By now, completely familiar with the routine, I motioned for my sister to follow me as we were ordered to search for a source of water. Eventually, we found a small swamp some distance from the campsite. The water was brown with filth and decay, its primary function was as a breeding ground for mosquitos. Continued use of this source for drinking and cooking would inevitably lead to disease as I had learned from my prior experiences.

Apparently, even Angka recognized the futility of this site because after ten days we were told that we would be returning to our former camp near Ksour. My sister and I heard this news with unrestrained joy since this meant an opportunity to again help our mother.

That evening when we had arrived at our former camp, we immediately began to plan our next trip to our mother's hut. We knew of course that risks were still involved in those secret meetings, but there had been so many changes over the last 10 days, that the possibility of discovering our absence was remote.

Two days later, we found our opportunity and made our way through the jungle to our mother's hut. No sooner had we entered the town than we became aware of a major change in the community. There were people in the streets and a less repressed atmosphere than we had remembered. When we finally reached our mother, she welcomed us with a great smile anxious to share her good news. In the two weeks that we had been gone, the town had indeed gone through a major change. The previous town leader, a cruel and ignorant woman, and in my eyes the worst of all Angka guards that I had met, had been replaced by a new leader who seemed to be less openly hostile then the previous leader. At least she promised more food and water to increase the food ration especially for the elderly, most of whom were in an extremely fragile condition, including my mother. I privately responded to this news with skepticism having heard similar promises before. But I hid these feelings to myself and hoped that this time there would be some measure of humanity remaining in our captors. To add to our joy, Angka permitted my brother Thouch and Navy to marry.

Over the next week, conditions gradually did improve although I was still gravely concerned for my mother's welfare. The next week, more encouraging news occurred. Our prior despised gang leader, the woman who had been the leader of the single women's group and who had sentenced me to two and a half years of slave labor and who was directly responsible for the deaths of many girls and young women was also forced to engage in field work.

In the midst of the continuing improvement in our conditions, my mother suddenly became very sick with a high fever and a generally weakened condition.

We knew that we would shortly be ordered to leave again but my sister and I also knew that if we left my mother now, she would not survive more than a few days. We agreed that we had no choice but to plead our case with the new group leader, allowing one of us to stay with her until she recovered.

I will never forget my sister's words that day. She was one year older than I, only 13, and still impaired from her earlier condition, but ready to do what many older men or women would not have the courage to do. She insisted that I must stay with our mother because I had suffered enough and that I must be given some relief from these experiences. She told me it was now her turn to work in the fields and I must use this time to recover my strength and to help our mother through her illness.

My sister's courage now served as the incentive for me to overcome my own fears. The next day, I went to our new group leader's quarters and pleaded my case. I promised that if I was granted permission to stay in town with my mother until she recovered that I would return to the fields. To my great surprise she approved my request and issued me the necessary papers. Upon my return to our work area, my sister and I started to pack my belongings since I was to leave immediately. When I was ready, we looked at one another with great love and devotion. There was no need for words. We both knew the enormous sacrifice she was making. Then, our eyes wet with tears, we said goodbye, and I walked out of the camp.

For the first time in many months, I made my way to my mother's hut in broad daylight without fear of being caught in a punishable offense. It was a journey made with a mixed heart. I looked forward to the opportunity to help my mother in her illness and to help her get better as she had done for me so often. At the same time, I kept reviewing in my mind's eye, the image of my sister waving goodbye to me, perhaps never to see her again.

I arrived at Ksour and immediately went to the town leader's house to show her my pass. She acknowledged my papers and told me to go directly to my mother and not to go anywhere else. I was only too happy to comply with her instructions and I raced to my mother's hut. She came out to greet me, a look of complete surprise on her face since she had thought her two youngest daughters had been forced to leave indefinitely. I explained to her what had happened and I could tell that she experienced that strange combination of emotion which all of us went through on such occasions, relief and joy on the one hand, sadness and concern on the other. But my first priority was her condition which had worsened since I last saw her. She was weak from starvation and burning with fever, and I knew that our decision for one of us to take care of her was the correct one. Over the next several days, my life fell into a new routine. Although I was permitted to care for my mother, I was also required to work in the town, which involved various odd jobs that were ordered on a daily basis. I was one of eight children who, for different reasons, had been given permission to remain with our families rather than work in the fields which had claimed so many lives.

Each day, as my schedule permitted, I would search the jungle for roots and herbs that my mother had told me had medicinal properties. As crude as these substances were, within a few days, her fever broke and she showed signs of recovering.

During this time, my sister, Chan, came to see us as often as she could, using the same strategy that I had shown her, making her way through the jungle at night to my mother's hut. This was our one small measure of respite from the nightmare that was still continuing under Angka. We knew, of course, that our time together would soon end, but we clutched on to every precious moment we could. One night, however, the inevitable happened. My sister came to us, weak and exhausted, her eyes red and swollen from tears. I knew before she told us the bad news because it had happened to me so often. That day the Angka leader had informed her group that they would be moving to a new field the next day. The women were frightened, not knowing where they would be going or how long they would be gone. Their fright turned to terror when rumors circulated that they would be taken to the Thailand border and forced to plant and harvest potatoes.

That night we slept together, perhaps the last time we would be allowed to do so. I tried to comfort her as best I could expressing a message of hope that I wasn't sure I believed myself.

The time came early the next morning for her to return to her camp. We were all exhausted from a sleepless night of strained emotions. My mother could not hide her despair at the prospect of seeing another child forced to leave for the work camps, perhaps never to see her again. We stood at the front of the hut as Chan turned to walk down the path into the jungle. She stopped to look back, waving to us with an expression of hopelessness and then she disappeared from view. It was one of the ever-increasing images that would never leave my mind.

We were given little time to grieve her departure. Shortly after Chan left, we learned that a number of young men from the single men's group had arrived at the town hospital. We heard that they were near death from the cruel conditions to which they had been exposed. I asked my mother if I should go to the hospital to see if my youngest brother, Thoeun, was in the boy's group. She agreed but warned me to be careful especially with what I might say to the guards.

I hurried to the hospital and as I approached the building, I heard the sound of voices yelling in pain. The sound was a frightening one, and I was reluctant to continue my search. Still, I had promised my mother, and I was determined to uncover any information I could about my brother.

As I reached the hospital, I saw the guards dragging boys into the hospital, all of whom were screaming in great pain. I approached the group to get a closer look at the faces of the boys. But now, I was hoping that my brother, Thoeun, was not part of this group, given their terrible condition and their cruel treatment by Angka.

I noticed one boy of about 14 who looked familiar. He was in great pain, but as I approached him we recognized one another, and he indicated a willingness to speak.

Although his speech was labored and he was gasping for breath, he told me that he had been a member of my brother, Thoeun's group, and that they had been living and working together for the last two years. He told me that my brother was alive and in the same camp that he had come from yesterday. He also told me that before he left, his group had been told they would be moved to the same camp to which my sister, Chan, was going. He, along with the other boys in the hospital, had been too sick to make the trip and they had been brought here instead.

I returned home and told my mother what I had learned. We talked for a long time about what all of this meant. She knew that the work required would be hard, of course, but perhaps worst of all, she would lose contact with her children because of the distance. Once again she would be sorely tried during a time when she could only hope for the best for her family. For myself, considering everything that had happened, these experiences were all too confusing. There were many questions that came to mind, but no answers.

The next day as I walked to the edge of town in search of food, I noticed an old wooden wagon in the distance being pulled by a cow. As the wagon approached the town, I realized that there was a man sitting in the wagon and curiously, the wagon was full of vegetables. I immediately ran to the man and I asked him where the vegetables were from and where he was going with them. He said that he had been instructed to transport the vegetables from a men's work camp in the jungle and to deliver them to the official cooks in the town. When I heard the news that a men's group was planting vegetables I thought instantly that this might have a special meaning for us. I ran home to share this information with my mother, and she agreed that this could be the work group to which my father had been assigned. I told her that the man said he was returning to the work group tomorrow morning and I realized that this could be an opportunity for me to find out if my father was indeed part of this work group. By this point in time, I had not seen my father in over two years.

First, she was strongly opposed to my plan and pointed out all the possible risks. But nothing would deter me from my intention and she finally agreed to let me go providing I was given permission from the town leader. By now I had learned the mentality of Angka, and when I asked the town leader for permission she agreed, assuming that I had made the request out of my interest in helping the man collect and move the vegetables.

We left early the next morning. I was still, after all, and despite countless hardships, a girl of 12, and anxious for any new adventure, particularly if this meant helping my family. My guide proved to be a kind and interesting man who told me a great deal about the working conditions of the camp site that was our destination. The more he described the circumstances, the more I was convinced that I would find my father there.

As we slowly made our way through the jungle I began to experience a sense of peacefulness and serenity that I had not known for many months. Each step took me further from the horrors of the work camp and into a land of sights and sounds that had a magical hypnotic quality to it. How wonderful it would be if at the jungle's end I was brought forth into another time and place where the nightmare was over and my family was completely reunited once again. Reality, of course, yielded a much ruder outcome.

We finally arrived at the men's work camp late in the day only to find that the workers were still in the field. I climbed down off the cart and thanked my elderly friend and turned to search for my father. My presence created something of a stir among the men since they were not accustomed to seeing a young girl in their midst. But I moved quickly from one group to another stopping for nothing but information. Suddenly, I was caught short, stunned at the sight of my brother, Thom, the second oldest sibling in my family. I didn't recognize him at first because he was much darker now from working in the sun and he had lost considerable weight which made him appear to be ten years older than I remembered. With a mixture of joy and amazement he looked hard at me as if to make certain that he was not dreaming.

I knew he wanted to hug me as I did him, but our greeting was restrained so as not to arouse a response from the guards. When we were able to speak, I asked about our father and his smiling response told me all I wanted to know. He told me that our father was indeed in this group, that they had been working closely together all this time and that he would take me to see him immediately. We walked to my father's hut which was located in the middle of a large melon field and made of sticks and grass which he had collected from the field. My father's job was to care for the plants and to protect the fruit from the animals. Thom and I sat down in the hut and waited for our father to return. Suddenly, we heard someone approaching the hut and my heart started beating rapidly with excitement. And then it happened, my father entered the hut and we were face-to-face for the first time in over two years. He also looked older and his face was drawn, his knees now larger than his head from starvation causing him to stumble as he walked toward me. His physical appearance shocked me and brought tears to my eyes. I hugged his fragile body with all of my strength never wanting to let go and we held each other for a long time.

I stayed with him in the hut that night informing him of everything I could, down to the tiniest detail. When I got to the most recent events, staying with my mother and my sister, and Chan volunteering to take my place in the fields, he grew silent and his face took on a worried look. It was the same expression I had seen on my mother's face whenever she thought about what might be happening to any of us.

That night, when we were alone and my father had checked to make sure that no Angka guards were in the area, he motioned for me to be silent and crept over to an area of the hut where he had obviously hidden something. Checking again to insure our safety, he knelt down before me and opened his hand to reveal a tiny mouse that he had skinned. I drew back in aversion, but he built a small fire and roasted the mouse on a spit. When it was cooked he urged me to eat it, pleading that it was safe and would provide nourishment. As great as my revulsion, I could not refuse his gesture and I swallowed it whole, fighting against the gagging sensation that it caused. A great smile crossed his face and then, with an expression of complicity he uncovered a second treasure, a piece of melon that he had somehow managed to hide from the guards. This, of course, was an act punishable by death, and as we ate it, the juices running down chins, I thought it was the sweetest piece of fruit I had ever eaten in my life.

Afterward, sitting and talking late into the night, we heard wild dogs barking nearby. Sensing my fear of animals which had remained with me since those nights my friend and I had crept through the jungle to visit our mothers, my father uncovered a hatchet which he had also hidden from the guards. He told me that he kept it at hand while he worked, but the true meaning of that gesture was the old sense that he would always protect me from harm.

The next morning, I had to leave at daylight since I would be returning alone through the jungle and my father wanted me to reach my mother's hut before dark. As I prepared to leave, the tears flowing freely, he hugged me and handed me a small bundle. It contained a small melon that I was to tell my mother he had picked especially for her.

Although I was only 12, I was by now an experienced jungle traveler. I could recognize the difference between safe sounds and those that might be associated with danger. Travelling alone through the jungle was no longer a fearful experience; in fact, I took special delight in hearing the wind rustling through the leaves, the birds calling to one another, these were all reassuring sounds of nature signifying that, at least here, away from Angka control, nothing had changed.

By the time I reached my mother's hut, it was late afternoon. She greeted me anxiously awaiting the news of her husband and fearing the worst. But my broad smile gave me away. Before I could even say anything she knew instinctively from my expression that her husband was alive. When I told her of my experience including having seen my brother, Thom, she was delighted beyond words. But I saved my best surprise for last. Making sure that we could not be seen, I opened the bundle that my father had given me and showed her the melon. Her eyes opened wide and I knew she couldn't have been more pleased with this humble gift than if I had brought great riches. No words were exchanged, but I could tell what this gesture from my father meant to her.

We ate the melon that night, relishing every bite as much for what it represented of earlier times as for its own sweetness. My mother wouldn't stop asking me about my father and my brother and so I repeated over and over every detail of my visit with them. I thought of the risk my father had taken for this small gesture which he knew would mean so much to my mother. I thought of how we were all making sacrifices for one another in an attempt to express our need to maintain the family. This was the source of our strength and it would survive the brutality and the indignities of Angka. My mother only smiled at my sentiments and she said simply, that she only wanted for our family to be together again, safe and unharmed.

Suddenly we heard noises outside and we hurried to hide the remaining piece of melon. As we listened in silence, both of us holding our breath we knew that it was Chhlob, the Angka group responsible for spying on the residents of the town. The noise stopped as suddenly as it started and Chhlob apparently moved off, having heard nothing suspicious. When we were sure that it was safe, my mother and I went outside and we spent the rest of the night lying in silence looking up into a dark sky with a multitude of shining stars. It had been a long time since either one of us had tried to enjoy the single serenity of a quiet night. By now, our lives in Phnom Penh were a fading memory. Now it seemed as if we were in a foreign country, a world which only offered pain and suffering. All we could do was make every effort to survive from one day to the next.

10

My mother and I and my 2-year old niece lived in this manner, surviving each day with the knowledge that my father and Thom were still alive and that perhaps we would see one another again soon. With the start of the rainy season, however, we began to encounter new problems. The great lake called Tonle Sab which was near the town soon began to rise and it was only a matter of time before it would overflow its banks and flood the fields and the town.

Each day, as more fields flooded, making field work impossible, the men's groups were ordered to return to the town. At the same time, Angka officials failed to recognize the danger to livestock and food supplies. A good example of their continued incompetence and inefficiency.

To my mother and me and the other women of the town, the heavy rains represented a mixed blessing with the threat of flooding on the one hand, coupled with the increasing possibility that our respective family members including my father and my two older brothers would soon be with us.

The day of their arrival finally came, but there was hardly any time to rejoice. First, we were dismayed by their haggard appearance. Secondly, the people of the town were panic-stricken. Several huts had already flooded out and no one knew where to turn for safety. Moreover, Angka now informed us that there were no food supplies available and that we would have to make do on our own. Death by starvation was, once again, a very real prospect.

True to form, any time there was a crisis of this nature, Angka were concerned only for their own survival, even if everyone else in their charge perished. I was ordered to leave the town along with nine other girls my age to move to higher ground in order to help protect their livestock. One guard was assigned to us to ensure that we would comply with our instructions.

By now, many of the paths in the town were under water and as we made our way to higher ground, we had to wade through swiftly moving currents, sometimes up to our waists in water. This was a terrifying experience and we had to grasp one another for support as we made our way to the new camp. We each had five pounds of rice that was to sustain us for at least a month until the water subsided. We finally reached the top of the hill where the animals were secured in pens. Our guard instructed us to make a raft for use in transporting food from the hill to Angka quarters in the town. Fortunately, there was a dead tree about 60 meters high and about 1/2 meter in thickness nearby which served the purpose. We cut the tree into one meter lengths and banded the sections together to make a raft that would carry three of us at a time. I located some bamboo that I cut into a pole which would enable us to move the raft through the water. During the time I was engaged in these activities, I was constantly thinking about my family back in the town and what I could do to help their situation. I had noticed a large number of banana trees partially submerged under water on the side of the hill, and I began to consider how I might bring some of the fruit to my family. Our guard inadvertently provided me with the means by telling me that I was to make the first delivery to town along with two other girls. That night, under cover of darkness, I made my way to the raft and slowly slipped into the water. It was very deep and cold, and the swirling currents increased my anxiety. Nevertheless, I managed to maneuver the raft next to the banana trees. My intention was to grasp the bananas and then tie them to the underside of the raft, but I had failed to account for the trees moving in the current as well as the difficulty involved in stabilizing the raft. Time and again, I would reach over the side of the raft and clutch the trees only to be forced away from my objective. After what seemed like an eternity, I succeeded in grasping several bunches of the bananas and bringing them to the surface. I placed them on the raft. I made my way back with the raft to where it had first been secured, and I tied the bananas to the underside of the raft.

Breathless and exhausted from the ordeal, I slipped back to my sleeping area without having aroused anyone and laid down to recover from fright. Sleep was out of the question after having been at such an emotional peak during the entire time. This was followed by the growing realization that my life was in danger if the Angka guard discovered what I had done.

The next morning, I completed my task of feeding the animals as quickly as I could. Without arousing any suspicion, I related this to our guard and told her I was ready to make the trip to town with the other two girls. She agreed and instructed us to return within an hour.

We maneuvered the raft through the water as quickly as possible. It was obvious that the water level was continuing

to rise and I wondered how the people in the town were deal-
ing with the mounting crisis.

When we reached my family's hut, I knew something was
different from when I left, but I couldn't quite put my finger
on the reason. I was surprised to see my father outside of the
hut. He was struggling at some task while standing in water
up to his waist. I yelled to him and when he saw me
approaching on the raft he registered a look of complete confusion. Surely this must have been an utterly unexpected
scene that would require some explanation for him to comprehend. We tied the raft to a nearby tree and when I asked
him why the hut looked different, he told me he had raised
the floor off its base four times to keep it above the rising
water. Then I told him we were on the raft to bring food to
Angka in the town. Disregarding the risk, I quickly described
what I had done the night before and that the bananas I
brought for them were lashed to the underside of the raft. As
soon as he realized the gist of my account, he jumped into the
water, swam to the raft, and dove under it. It was no easy task
for him to free the bananas from under the raft since the water
was deep and the fruit was water soaked and heavy and he
was, of course, concerned that he would be seen engaged in
a criminal activity. As he struggled to bring the bananas to the
hut, my mother appeared at the entrance and, reaching down,
she helped my father carry the heavy load into the hut. The
look of joy on her face at this unexpected benefit meant post-
poning starvation for at least a short time. This was soon
replaced with an expression of alarm when she realized the
risks I had taken in bringing the bananas to them.

After all was said and done and I understood the magnitude
of my behavior, I concluded that if I had to do it again, I would

still do the same thing tomorrow. There was now no prospect of any food in the town for the inhabitants either by supply or through the people's own efforts. A number of men, including my father, tried to catch fish in the flooded town but without success. I knew if the roles were reversed any one of my family members would sacrifice their own life for my own. Watching my parents decide how the food I brought them could be used to stave off starvation gave me a feeling of great satisfaction.

That night, after returning to the campsite while lying in my sleeping area, I reviewed the events of the last 24 hours in my mind. The fact that I had outwitted Angka while helping my family only increased the positive feeling of my achievement. Once again, I realized that despite all of their resources and all of their attempts to force their will on us even to the point of death, one person, even a young girl could, in some small way, defy these cruel and corrupt people. It was now common knowledge among the Cambodians that the Angka had implemented a systematic campaign to exterminate the populace. Although the future would bring great pain and suffering, each of us would have to resist this effort in our own way.

The next morning we were told by our guard that it would be our responsibility to deliver food to all of the neighboring towns and villages. We were given the names of the officials who would receive and distribute the food in each case. As we carried out our assignment we learned that all of these communities had also experienced great suffering and were on the edge of starvation.

Several days later, much to everyone's surprise, a large boat arrived at our town with a large store of food supplies for Angka. After the food had been unloaded, I was told that three other girls and I were to ride with the boat upstream and try to find additional food for the Angka's livestock. I was given a 24-hour pass and told to board immediately. Consequently, I had no opportunity to inform my parents of my new assignment. Early the next morning, the boat left its mooring and we started a slow journey up the river. The trip was a quiet, peaceful interlude in our hectic, crisis-laden lives and it gave us time to wonder about our circumstances. None of us could have anticipated the terror we would experience in the next 24 hours.

We arrived at our destination late in the afternoon, a relatively large town that had been spared the devastation of the flood experienced by the villages downstream. The four of us were led to the Angka leader who reviewed our papers and informed us that we would have to wait for morning before we could get any food. This was a matter of some concern for us since our instructions required us to return in 24 hours, and we had only one day's food ration, but there was nothing for us to do but comply. We soon all discovered that most of the children of Ksour had been brought here and we became convinced that we would also be kept captive in this town.

The next morning we appeared at Angka headquarters and we were each given a basket of corn to take back with us. We then returned to where the boat had docked the day before only to find that it was not there. After some discussion, we decided to wait for it, assuming that we would be picked up for our return. As the day wore on with no sign of the boat we became increasingly frightened about returning on time. By the middle of the afternoon we frantically began to consider our options. If we were to make our way on our own, we would have to march through a heavily wooded field for some distance and negotiate through the water at those points where the undergrowth proved to be impassable. Since I was the only one of the four of us who was unable to swim, this was a terrifying prospect for me. On the other hand, we also knew that we would be subject to severe punishment if we violated our passes. This added to the concern that if we didn't leave soon, we might be confined here permanently. Finally, the other three girls prevailed upon me to start on our way with the assurance that they would help me whenever we were in deep water.

We made our way through the undergrowth and, all too soon, discovered that the only way to continue was by wading through the water. This proved to be as dangerous and treacherous for my colleagues as it was for me. We were soon wading waist high through the water unsure of every step, sometimes struggling against a strong current. We clutched each other's hands with total desperation, convinced that anyone or all of us would be swept away at any moment. To add to our consternation, the corn that we carried was now beginning to weigh us down as it became sodden with water.

As we struggled on in the cold water, using our body in unfamiliar ways, every muscle began to ache with excruciating intensity. In particular, my knees felt swollen with pain. To add to our agony, the sun began to set adding the terror of darkness and the loss of our bearings.

Stumbling, confused and in pain, hope of our survival began to dwindle. We were now all crying hysterically, slipping under the water from time to time as our footing gave way. Each time we would surface, gasping for air, shivering in the cold, our clothes totally sodden and becoming an extra burden. Still we continued on, offering encouragement and support to one another and clutching a fallen comrade for dear life whenever one of us dropped under the water. Exhausted and frightened beyond belief, convinced that death was imminent the next time we stumbled, we searched desperately for any sign of light. We continuously cried out in the darkness hoping perhaps that a fisherman or Angka guard would come to our assistance.

I thought of my family, my parents, my siblings throughout this ordeal. How ironic to have survived the death camps, starvation and other forms of punishment, only to die by drowning while attempting to bring food to animals.

After perhaps five to six hours, we suddenly heard the sound of whistling in the darkness. As the sound became louder and more distinct, we realized that this was in response to our cries and was heading in our direction.

Out of the dark we could make out the form of a man in a rowboat. By now we were shouting and screaming for him to save us. When he drew near and we realized that we had been saved, we all started talking simultaneously in a rush of words, trying to explain our pitiful condition.

Finally, after he had helped us into his boat and we were able to gain control over our emotional state, we told him of our experience and what we had been assigned to do.

His calm and understanding demeanor served to reassure us. He told us that we were only a short distance from our destination and, true to his word, we reached the town shortly thereafter, cold, exhausted, and still at an emotional pitch, but alive. I never knew the man's name who saved us, I never saw his face because of the darkness, nor is there any explanation for what he was doing or why he was there when he found us, but I shall never forget his reassuring manner.

Thanks to this kind gentleman who appeared in the night at the height of our distress, I had cheated death one more time. How many more crises would I encounter before the nightmare was over either through the end of the Angka regime or through my demise?

When we left the boat we had to climb the hill to reach our sleeping quarters. As I started the climb with the other girls, I suddenly collapsed in pain, unable to walk. Now that the crisis of wading through water had passed, I realized that something was desperately wrong with my legs which were swollen with pain. With the help of the other girls I crawled to my bunk aware of the fact that this was a serious problem resulting from the rigors of wading through the water. The next morning, still in great pain, I hobbled as best I could to our guard's quarters and pleaded with her to be taken to my mother for treatment. At first, she was unconvinced of the severity of my condition, but as the day progressed and the pain and swelling worsened, she finally agreed to my plea.

By the time the raft that I was on reached my mother's house, it was plain that I was suffering from a severe infection that was out of control. My mother told me that fluid was draining out of open sores all over my legs. She left immediately to find herbs and other substances to treat the infection. This was difficult and time-consuming since much of the terrain was now under water. Finally she returned after about two hours and started to apply the herbs to the affected areas. Slowly, my condition improved and by the next day the swelling went down. Once again, as she had so many times before, my mother's wisdom and care served to heal me and within a week I was able to walk again.

Over the next several months, Angka allowed us to live

together and our daily lives became routine. By November the water had receded, however, once again we were faced with severe food shortages. Virtually no livestock or vegetation had survived the flood and even the water was unsafe to drink. In a short time, the people were experiencing starvation, many of us resorted to eating frogs, rats, and snakes, a circumstance I had already experienced on several prior occasions.

The lack of food and the resulting starvation did not deter Angka. We were all ordered back to the fields and the work continued unabated. This circumstance only accelerated our desperate condition. People were either dying outright or on the edge of death. Our skin became translucent with bones clearly showing underneath. As our bodies coped with the absence of nourishment, our stomachs became distended and our heads appeared to be out of proportion with the rest of our bodies. For most of us, our skin and the whites of our eyes turned yellow. We were truly a community of walking dead. Once again, I was on the threshold of death, but my mother recognized the condition. She mixed a potion of sour palm juice in which she had marinated a rusty nail for about eight days. She made me drink a small portion each day for about a week and gradually my skin returned to its normal condition.

One day, after about two months had passed my older brother, Than, suddenly appeared at my mother's house. From his frightened and agitated state, it was clear that he was in great distress. He told me quickly that he had escaped from the single men's group and that he had been hiding from Angka. I told him that this was a violation punishable by death and he responded by saying that he would rather die than continue to suffer as he had the past three-and-one-half years.

We decided that he should stay with us until tomorrow in order to rest and decide where he would go next, since it was just a matter of time before the guards came searching for him in our hut. We didn't have long to wait, however, and that evening, while my mother was out of the hut, I spotted a guard from his group approaching our hut. He was no more than 18 with such an intense determined air about him, I knew instantly my brother was at great risk. I rushed to warn my brother to hide out in back and then turned to the front to intercept the guard. I could tell from his expression and the anger in his voice that my worst fears for my brother's safety were warranted. It was clear there would be no sympathy from this man.

He asked me if I had seen my brother and I responded that no one had been there all day. He obviously rejected my answer and hurried to the back of the hut and found my brother crouching behind some shrubbery. Rushing and shouting at my brother, he ordered Than to return immediately with him to the men's group. My brother grabbed a hatchet that he had hidden and, brandishing it with a menacing gesture, warned the guard that he would kill him rather than return to the fields. The guard stepped back several paces and then, spotting a large sturdy bamboo branch, grabbed it and rushed at my brother. I screamed at the guard and fell at his feet, begging him not to kill my brother. I clutched at his leg with desperation, hoping to give my brother some time to defend himself. The guard kicked me away and warned me that I was also in danger if I interfered. My brother reacted as I had hoped and ran off into the jungle. As the guard moved to follow him, I continued to struggle with him clutching any part of his body my hands could grab while I begged over and over for my brother's safety. The guard continued to kick me until he finally freed himself from me. Shouting a warning to me, he ran off into the jungle after my brother.

I lay where I had fallen, sobbing hysterically, emotionally spent and wondering if my brother would be dragged back by the guard to face his punishment.

Within minutes the guard returned alone, his face contorted with anger and hatred. He looked at me with such menace that I shall never forget the expression on his face, but I had succeeded in helping my brother escape.

My mother returned to our house a short while later and when she saw my frightened state and the bruises on my body from where the guard had kicked me, she became terribly frightened herself. I described the incident with my brother and the guard and she knew it was just a matter of time before Angka returned to search for him again.

I told her that I would wait until dark and search for Than to bring him food and water. That night, I ran through the jungle, calling his name out as softly as I could. After searching a short while, I heard him returning my call and found him hiding in the top of a large tree. I reassured him that it was safe and he jumped down next to me, frightened and exhausted. While he was rapidly eating the food I brought him, I urged him to escape this area and to join our father's group. He agreed to do so, embraced me and disappeared into the jungle.

The next morning, the same guard who had threatened my brother returned to our house. His face contorted in hatred, he represented everything cruel and barbaric about Angka. After searching the house and the grounds he left abruptly shouting threats and warnings.

I knew this was only a temporary solution to my brother's problem since joining my father's group was safe only if his presence remained undiscovered. If Angka found him, both he and my father would be executed. Consequently, I was not surprised when he quietly stole back into our hut several days after his escape to say goodbye and to inform us of his plans to seek refuge in a distant part of the country. He told us that my sister-in-law Savvy's two sisters, Vanna and Limang, who were hiding in her parents' hut were joining him in his escape attempt which increased the risk for all three of them. Later that night, we quietly said our goodbyes and with one quick backward glance he was out the door and into the jungle.

My mother and I stayed up late after they left. Even though we knew this was the only decision, it was one more blow to our already fragile circumstances. We both cried as we thought of Than's escape, knowing full well the terrible consequences if he was captured. In fact, to our knowledge no one had ever successfully escaped, and all of us had witnessed executions of those who had been caught. Now, my mother had to add this burden to her grief over my sister, Chan, who had taken my place in the fields and the complete absence of my oldest sister, Chantha, who we still had not heard from in over three years. Now, three of her children might be lost forever and it was more than she could bear. I did my best to comfort her that night, but it was difficult for me to conceal my own deep anxieties about their fate.

11

It was now late fall of 1978, three months from when my brother, Than, said goodbye and left the area out of fear for his life. Of all the bitter times we had endured under the Angka regime, this was perhaps the most difficult. Not only did we have to deal with the fact that members of our family were scattered to parts unknown, but the mere struggle to survive grew grimmer by the day. Once again, we were faced with the necessity to find enough food to simply live through each day. The dead and the dying mounted on a daily basis with little regard for our welfare on the part of Angka. We were totally left up to our own devices, seeking sources of nourishment from our surroundings. Periodic reports of more food shortly being available came to our attention, but who knew if we could survive even if they were based on truth?

At the same time and of a more exciting nature, rumors of an armed and growing resistance to Angka also began to circulate among the townspeople. Initially, the news was passed on secretly and one had to be extremely cautious that this wasn't another trick on the part of Angka to root out their enemies. But the rumors soon began to be discussed more openly and included reports of actual fighting in the jungles of Cambodia, lending them the stamp of credibility and it became easier each day to believe in them. Slowly, at first, but with

gradually increasing likelihood, a sense of hope and excitement began to infuse our daily lives. There was, of course, an
equally growing concern as my mother pointed out. If there
was indeed an emerging armed resistance to the regime, what
was to stop Angka from retaliating against the field workers
and the townspeople who were totally vulnerable to their
anger?

In the face of these conflicting factors we tried to maintain
a normal routine while continuing our constant struggle to find
food.

It was at this time that I was instructed by my guard to join
with four other girls to bring the remaining chickens under our
care to the men's group. This meant that I would once again
have an opportunity to see my second oldest brother, Thom.
Naturally, I was overjoyed at the prospect. We left early the
next day and arrived at the camp after about an 18-hour hike
through the jungle. When we arrived, we came upon the usual
customary camp scene: tired, emaciated young and older
men, working the fields in an almost robot-like manner. I
found my brother, Thom, first only to discover, much to my
great surprise, that his wife, Savvy, was working with him. He
informed me that several days earlier, a small group of women
had arrived to help the men and happily for him, his wife was
among them. Her totally unexpected arrival at Thom's camp
was another one of those small miracles that kept happening
to us just often enough to give us hope in our effort to survive.

I spent that night with my brother and sister-in-law. Thom
told me that rumors of the resistance movement had reached
his camp several weeks ago and that, in fact, during the last
several days, the camp was quietly visited at night by men

who identified themselves as members of the resistance asking for food to bring back to their colleagues. They were always polite and understanding on those occasions when there was nothing to be shared. Nevertheless, their presence increased the risks for everyone in the camp and my brother told me I must return to our mother as soon as possible the next day and not to leave town for any reason. He added that he and his wife were planning to join us within the next several days. Later, after we fell asleep, the sound of footsteps outside the hut woke us and my brother ran immediately to the entrance while gesturing for us to remain inside and not to talk. When Savvy and I glanced outside, we noticed a number of workers including my brother clustered around several men talking in hushed tones. They were collecting small bags of rice to take with them back to the jungle. They also had a radio with them, and it was clear everyone in the group was listening and responding enthusiastically to the news that was being broadcast.

My brother quickly returned and, first making certain that we were alone, told us in a state of great excitement what they heard. This was a live broadcast from Phnom Penh informing the audience that the Vietnamese Army was engaged in combat with Angka near the capital and that many of the Angka guards were actually surrendering. This was staggering news to all of us and we could scarcely conceal our excitement as well as our fear. The magnitude of this circumstance, in particular, the involvement of the Vietnam Army was totally incomprehensible and an event that no one had ever considered. We sat in stunned silence trying to understand the meaning of these developments and to appreciate the growing possibility that this might mean the end of the hated regime.

Early the next morning, the other girls and I started off on our return back to town. The march was remarkable for the fact that we walked in complete silence, each one of us reluctant to talk about the reports that had circulated like wildfire the night before. Our total silence was more striking than anything that could have been expressed in words.

When we entered the town, my first reaction was that nothing had changed. The townspeople were working just as they always had and I guessed that the stunning news of last night had not reached here yet. As soon as I was able to get away, I ran to my mother's hut to share what I had learned about the hostilities between the Vietnamese and the Angka regime. Predictably, her reaction was to think of how these events would impact on our family and she said we must all now prepare for trouble.

We wondered why she responded in this manner, rather than rejoicing at the prospect of freedom from Angka. Sometime later, she told us that one of her women friends overheard two guards discussing the fact that both my father's and my brother's past had been discovered and that they were scheduled for execution on their return to town.

My mother prepared to spend that night in prayer, asking for divine assistance in protecting her husband and children from the great danger that she was convinced was soon to come. As she knelt, deep in her meditation, the door to the house opened, and my sister, Chan, walked in and embraced us. My mother and I were stunned since we had heard nothing of her circumstances from the day she walked off to take my place in the fields three months earlier. Her sudden appearance, although weak and emaciated, was as if my mother's prayers had been miraculously answered. We fell into each other's arms crying and laughing hysterically.

We spent the remainder of that night happily rejoicing in her safe return and talking of the major events that were happening all over Cambodia. Chan said that although she wasn't aware of all of the circumstances, the Angka guards had suddenly left her camp two days ago and as soon as she and the other girls realized what had happened they seized on this opportunity to escape. While on the road, she and 15 of the other girls stopped and asked a man driving a dump truck if he would help them, not knowing if he could be trusted or whether he would simply deliver them back to Angka. Fortunately, he agreed and they piled into the back of the truck. On the road back to town, Chan said the roads, usually well-patrolled, were deserted as if Angka had vanished overnight. When we asked her about Thoeun, who was working in the men's group in the same area, she said she had no information as to his whereabouts, but that apparently everyone who had been held captive in the camp, had scattered into the jungle.

The next morning we were abruptly aroused by shouts and screams in the neighborhood. We cautiously looked out of the windows and saw Angka guards and military personnel running in all directions, weapons in their hands scattering in the jungle. Our first thought was that they were preparing to kill all of the townspeople and then disappear. My mother quickly led Chan and me behind the hut where we hid behind some bushes. Signaling us to be quiet, we lay there trembling in silence wondering what would happen next.

The shouts of the soldiers slowly faded away as they ran off and we continued to remain where we were, scarcely breathing. Soon, there was a complete and eerie silence. Even the hated town bell signaling the assembly for the work groups remained silent. Yet, we did not move for fear that any response on our part would bring Angka back. After about an hour, we cautiously made our way to the front of the hut where we could look onto the paths leading through the town. By now, others had also slowly began to leave their huts and gathered in the open to try to make sense of this confusing development. Could it be true that almost four years of brutality and deprivation had come to an end? It was almost too much for anyone to comprehend.

Then, gradually at first, but with a quickening pace, we began to grasp the reality of our circumstances. The guards had gone, if only temporarily, and we now had options that we could not have considered less than 24 hours earlier. Many of the people suggested that we leave immediately, in fear that Angka might return and kill everyone. A number of people actually gathered their few possessions and hastily left. But for us, that decision was far more complicated, since leaving might mean any chance of being reunited with my father and the other members of the family would be lost.

For this reason we decided to remain in the town at least until there was some more compelling necessity to leave. As we talked among ourselves for the first time in almost four years, we heard the sounds of airplanes approaching. They passed some distance away followed by the thud of explosions which we guessed to be targeted at Angka. If this were so, it would be almost too good to be true.

As the day wore on, events became even more confusing with some townspeople leaving, others returning, new faces joining those of us who stayed. Still we waited, not knowing for certain why or what was in store. But our eyes continued to search the dusty road leading into town, hoping for another miracle. And then it happened. Almost as if out of a dream, emerging from the crowd we recognized the familiar faces of my father and my brothers, Choeun and Thom, together with their wives and children making their way toward our hut. My mother and Chan and I screamed in delight as we rushed to hug them, scarcely knowing what to say. We were completely overcome by emotion, the tears flowing from each of us. Now, except for my sister, Chantha, and my brothers, Thouen and Than, who had escaped the Angka guard, our family was reunited for the first time in almost four years.

When we finally gained control over our emotions, we began to consider how to deal with our new circumstances. Although most of the town's people had left the area, we resolved not to leave until both missing brothers rejoined us. My father told us that we should pack our few possessions in order to be prepared to leave as soon as they arrived. My other brother, Thom, went to the food storage maintained by Angka and when he returned with enough rice, corn and sugar to provide us for several weeks, we realized once again, the extreme cruelty of our guards. In the face of utter starvation on the part of their captives, they had more food than they could possibly use themselves.

Now events began to happen so rapidly, we almost could not comprehend each new development. The very next day after my father and two brothers appeared, Thouen arrived, weak and tired from a trip of perhaps one hundred and fifty miles. We fell on him as we had our other family members and rejoiced in his survival.

Later that afternoon, after we had given thanks for our reunion and prayed for the survival of our other family members, we observed an exhausted Than slowly making his way on the path to the town. We rushed to greet him and to help him the rest of the way. Although his physical condition was desperate, we were of course, overjoyed that he had survived his ordeal. Now, finally, it was time to leave this horrible place that had been the scene of so much pain and suffering. I didn't care what the future held in store. I only knew that most of my family was together again and that I wanted to escape from here forever.

We started out on the road leading west to Battdambang, which was safer than continuing to stay in the jungle.

My father thought this would best serve our purpose since it was the second largest in Cambodia, it was within two days walking distance, and it was the city where my oldest brother, Choeun, once lived. We walked all day through the jungle, talking from time to time about our various experiences, trying to share memories with one another. We were all curious about my brother, Than, who had recently escaped capture by running into the jungle, intending to reach the border. He told us that he had made it only as far as the next town and was caught without a pass. Angka immediately chained him in a cage below ground. He was unable to move for days at a time, never seeing daylight. As his skin began to rot, he would surely have died, if the recent events hadn't driven off the guards. He was set free by the local townspeople and immediately left to find us again. We all marveled at the fact that, for whatever reason, we had each of us managed to survive various ordeals under extraordinary circumstances and now had reason to believe that the worst was over. Along with many other families on the march, we stopped to sleep that night in an open rice field with only the stars above us.

Ironically, this was one of the very rice fields that had been the scene of so much Angka brutality and we thought about the countless number of countrymen who had lost their lives under the regime. As crude as our beds were, we rejoiced in the fact that we were together and hopefully, free of Angka.

My father and brother, Thom, however, left nothing to chance and remained on guard that night armed with a knife and hatchet. There were other men in the group, similarly armed with crude weapons. We were not concerned over the threat of our neighbors but rather defending ourselves against the possibility of attack by Angka. Even though our arms would be no match for their weapons, one could sense a quiet but deep sense of resolution among the people. We would fight Angka with sticks and stones, if need be, rather than submit to them. We didn't have long to wait to test our determination.

Early the next morning as we gathered our possessions and prepared to continue our march, two men in Angka uniforms and carrying rifles suddenly emerged out of the jungle, screaming insults and threats at us. Aiming their rifles at us they demanded to know why we had left our work groups and, with murderous expressions ordered us to return to our assigned work camps. They apparently were unaware of the attack on Angka by the Vietnamese and considered us to be a band of traitors. Almost as if on cue, however, every person in the group stood up and with a show of their weapons challenged the two men, making it clear that some of us might die, but that they too would be killed. Even the women and children arose and started screaming threats and insults at them spontaneously. We raised our fists and started to move in their direction. Their reaction was immediate. Their eyes opened wide and with an expression of fear, they turned and ran off into the jungle. The people in the group, perhaps some 30 families turned to one another and with our fists raised and shouts of triumph, exacted some small measure of revenge on our hated captors. It was heartening to see them scurrying off like frightened animals.

Afterward we resumed our walk through the jungle without any further incident. We saw no signs of Angka anywhere which made us grateful to the Vietnamese Army although we still didn't understand the reasons for their intervention into Cambodia. As we drew closer to the city and the roads became more crowded, we also began to see men in military uniform. Our first reaction to this sight was one of concern, but we soon realized that they belonged to the Vietnamese Army and meant us no harm. Quite the contrary. We learned that as long as they were present, Angka would be nowhere in sight. That night we slept in a small town near Battdambang, secure in the knowledge that we were now under the protection of the Vietnam military.

The next day, a Vietnam officer gathered the people together and, using sign language, informed us that Angka was still a threat in the area, that the fighting was still going on and that we should all go to Battdambang province where we would be safe.

We followed his suggestion and continued our march to the town. By mid-morning we had reached the outskirts of Battdambang and were walking past the airport. It was obvious that this had been a center of the hostilities because of the craters left by the bombs and the debris scattered over the area.

Later that day we reached Thouch's wife Navy's house only to discover that it had been damaged by the fighting.

Nevertheless, it seemed that it was a safe place to stay. We remained there for a week, slowly recovering our strength and considering what our next move might be. The decision was made for us by a Vietnam official who informed us that they expected a counter-attack by Angka sometime soon and that we should leave the town or risk getting caught in the middle. We took his advice and quickly left the house, making our way to the suburbs. My father knew of an old temple outside Battdambang and he directed us there as a temporary stop. We built a small hut for shelter while we contemplated our next move. Food was once again becoming scarce and over the next several days, we would search the jungle surrounding the temple for anything that was available. We knew there were risks involved in this effort since Angka were still in the area and they had planted exploding traps everywhere which had already killed many people.

Nevertheless, as our circumstances became more desperate and nearby sources of food became depleted, we found ourselves foraging deeper and deeper into the jungle. More often than not my father and my brothers returned empty-handed from their search having been turned back by the Vietnamese because of the dangers to their safety. For this reason, my sister, Chan, and I were strictly forbidden to go off into the jungle. But, again, we were together and somehow endured these hardships.

12

We stayed in this location for several months living a hand-to-mouth existence, surviving as best we could in this manner. It was a time of instability for the whole country, while the two military factions continued their fighting. More people gathered in the temple area, and, each day would bring new faces to the site, while families searched for loved ones and tried to reestablish old ties. My mother now spent each day on the road or in front of our hut searching for my oldest sister, Chantha, who had been absent from us for over three and one-half years.

We all began to recognize that Chantha's absence was becoming a source of great anxiety to my mother and my father and brothers were determined to search for her. Since Chantha was last living in a town 200 miles from my grandmother's house, we would have to acquire a bicycle to get there, as short of walking this was the only means of transportation. Bicycles, however, were almost impossible to acquire and could only be purchased with gold, the one source of currency still valued in Cambodia. That left the next question of how to obtain the gold, since my mother had long ago bartered her jewelry for food. It was my brother, Thom, who finally suggested a possible solution to our dilemma. He had managed to hide a pair of highly valued U.S. sunglasses from Angka. This could be traded for a variety of things, including cotton yarn to be used for weaving a *Kraw Ma*, a type of towel, popular among our people, and worn around the neck for protection from the sun. The Kraw Ma, in turn, could be sold for enough gold to purchase two bikes. Without considering the actual feasibility of such an extraordinary plan, we all knew that at the very least, my mother would react to this favorably since the act of weaving the Kraw Ma would represent a direct effort on her part to continue the search for Chantha.

Within the next few days, my brother, Thom, returned to the hut with a large quantity of cotton yarn and my mother started to weave with it almost immediately. Over the next several months, working day and night, my mother and Chan continued to weave a series of Kraw Mas. Whenever she completed one, I would take the finished cloth to the center of town and trade it for food and gold. Finally, after three months of continued work, we had enough gold to purchase two bikes which two of my brothers would use to travel to the town where Chantha had been living.

The very next day Thom and Than left on their search, and we could only go on with our lives in the hope that they would return as soon as possible with news of our sister.

The days passed slowly as we waited for news from my brothers and sister. My mother prayed each day for their safety and for that of my father's mother who we hoped was still living in the same vicinity as my sister, Chantha. Meanwhile, we tried as best we could to reconstruct the lives we had led prior to the Angka takeover. Many Cambodians were heading toward the border with Thailand to trade gold for food. Others were returning to their hometowns and we also considered going back to Phnom Penh especially after learning that the regime had evacuated the former capital. But when we heard from refugees that our beautiful home had been destroyed in 1975 we no longer considered that as an option. Again, however, our first priority was my sister, Chantha's, welfare so we remained in our shelter outside the city of Battdambang.

About a month passed with still no word from my brothers. It was hard to maintain a normal routine, especially for my mother, while our anxiety continued to mount. Late one quiet afternoon there were six of us gathered in our hut while my mother was preparing a small amount of food for our evening meal. I walked outside for no particular reason but simply out of a sense of restlessness. As I glanced up the road leading to the west, I noticed two men on bicycles in the distance riding in my direction. As I continued to watch the approaching figures, it became obvious that one of the bikes had a second rider. My heart started beating rapidly at the thought that this might be my brothers, Thom and Than, returning with Chantha. I raced inside the house shouting for everyone to come and see the three people who were approaching. As we ran back out together we saw one of the most beautiful sights I had seen in four years. My two brothers had found my sister, Chantha, alive and well and were returning to rejoin the family. We ran to greet them, my mother embracing her daughter who had been separated from us for so long. Tears of happiness flowed from all of us. This was truly a miracle that after each of us had suffered so terribly for so long, our family was once again together. Our love for each other had outlasted the cruelty of Angka.

When we had a chance, my sister, Chantha, and I stopped and simply looked at one another to appreciate this moment.

She looked even prettier than I remembered her when I had last seen her. She told me how proud she was of me and that I had grown into a beautiful young woman. We smiled at one another and embraced again. Our gesture of love for one another spoke more than words could utter.

Later, as we shared our meal together Chantha told us of the events that had occurred during the past four years, when she and her husband Samouth had gone off to live with his parents. The same day they arrived in the village, Angka immediately ordered them to the fields. They were unable to meet Samouth's parents, and in fact, Chantha never saw Samouth again. Her last news of him was that he had died in the fields. During the time that she remained in this camp, she suffered from starvation and illness as we all did. After his death, she lived with his parents for several weeks when they were forced to move to a small farming area about 30 miles from our present location. When the Vietnamese invaded Cambodia, she went back to my grandmother's house hoping to find out about us. When she learned that we had also been forced to move, she assumed that we had all met our deaths. She had no other choice then but to remain with our grandmother, who was still alive, having somehow also survived the nightmare of the regime. My brothers found them and Chantha pleaded with her to join them in their return to us, but she declined, insisting instead that she would move in with her other son, my father's older brother, and live the rest of her life where she had always lived.

On their journey back, Chantha and my two brothers passed through the village of *Siemreab* which was the last residence of my mother's sister *Kong* and her husband and seven children. When they asked the villagers of my Aunts circumstances, they learned that the whole family had been executed in a massacre of the intellectuals, simply because her husband had been a school teacher. Kong was my mother's youngest sibling and the news left her paralyzed with grief.

Now, the only remaining link in the reconstruction of our family was my mother's mother and her younger brother who had lived together before the Angka coup and who had been lost to us since that time. Unfortunately, learning of their circumstances proved to be an impossible task and our efforts to find them was unsuccessful.

13

Over the next several weeks, our lives returned to some degree of normalcy. We were still faced with the long-term decisions of how and when to restore our lives, but the more immediate concern of avoiding starvation was a daily struggle. As a community of neighbors slowly evolved, we began to realize the magnitude of the Angka disaster. Each of us knew from our own circumstances of the cruelty and barbarism of Angka practices on an individual basis. But it wasn't until we began to share these experiences with others that a broader perspective emerged. Each time one of us described the horrors we had personally lived through, we learned there were others who had witnessed even crueller events. The worst were the reports of mass killings including babies and young children that had taken place throughout the country. In our own case, my father learned one of his older brother's sons, along with his wife and two children, had been executed by Angka on suspicion of their opposition to the regime. The other son starved to death in a work camp. In short, it was a time of great mourning and sadness for everyone. Not one family had been spared personal tragedy.

Slowly, however, our thoughts turned to the future. Many people were still heading toward Thailand although we had been told there was great danger in choosing this alternative. It was Thom who once again decided that we must determine the risks involved, particularly since his wife, Savvy, was pregnant and he wanted her to have the best care possible under the circumstances. He told us that he was planning to leave the next day to find a safe route to the border and that he would return for all of us as soon as he could. He left early the next morning with our prayers for his safe return.

We tried to busy ourselves with our daily routines, but we also spent each day looking up the road to the west which we knew Thom must take on his return. Two weeks passed quickly and, almost before we knew it, he was back in our household exhausted but safe. We gathered immediately to hear his news and after he had eaten and briefly rested, he described his experiences to us. He informed us that the journey through the jungle to Thailand was extremely difficult and dangerous. Angka forces still controlled sections of the route and they had no compunctions about killing anyone they encountered.   Moreover, they had planted explosive traps along a number of paths which had either killed or injured many refugees. In any event, he added, if we were to attempt to escape to Thailand we must do so soon since the fighting between the Vietnamese and Angka was escalating.   That night, as we all gathered to consider what Thom had said, we recognized that we had only two options: to remain here outside of Battdambang and slowly starve to death or to risk our lives to gain freedom by escaping to the border. Given these alternatives, we agreed to start the next day on the trail to Thailand.   Only my brother, Thouch, decided to remain in Cambodia in order to help his wife, Navy, now the oldest of her family since her parents had been killed by Angka, in her search for her seven brothers and sisters who at last word had scattered throughout the country. Although we knew this decision might mean we would never be together again, we understood his feelings and my mother said she would pray for their safety.

14

It was now early winter 1979. The decision to leave our beloved country was a difficult one. Many of the people at the camp were openly angry at us while we prepared to leave. They were convinced that peace would someday return to Cambodia and that we were betraying our heritage. For myself, I was confused by their behavior. So many people had been brutally murdered, families disrupted, towns and villages destroyed, our country totally devastated, that it seemed to me these people were denying the reality of our circumstances by holding on to the past. I knew, as young as I was, we had made the right decision. It didn't take us long to pack our meager possessions to prepare for the dangerous journey, and to leave the memories, both good and bad behind forever. That night I said goodbye to my country, my people, and the first fourteen years of my life.

We started early the next morning on what we hoped would be the last such journey of our lives. There were 13 of us including Choeun's and Kim Run's two children. We knew the walk would be hard and hoped to get as good a start as possible. Thom led the way, being careful to help his wife, Savvy, now in her seventh month, as much as possible. My Papa carried his youngest grand-daughter, Karin, on his shoulders to spare the little four year old the pain of the long walk. I was responsible for my five year old niece, Kara, helping her along as best as I could, playing games, asking questions, singing and in fact, anything to keep her mind off the difficult trip. Our pace was a slow one since Chantha was in great pain from sores on the bottom of her feet.

Each day we walked 18 hours struggling through dense jungle trails and an unforgiving terrain – sleeping when we could. From time to time, we came upon Vietnamese troops riding in trucks heading in all different directions. When they stopped to ask us for our destination, we simply indicated that we were heading to the next town to join up with family members. We knew if we told them we were heading to the border, they would have forced us to turn back.

We walked for seven days ending each night by sleeping under what little shelter we could find. When the day ended, we would fall to the ground, completely fatigued, our legs heavy, our bodies in pain. Yet, in some ironic way, the harsh circumstances imposed on us by Angka had actually prepared us for this journey.

On the seventh day of our trip, we reached a small town that was about 35 miles from the border. Here we joined a number of other families who were also attempting to leave Cambodia, all as desperate as we were to escape the horrors of Angka. We saw mothers holding infants, old men and women barely able to walk, children frightened and confused, all like us, praying for one chance to gain freedom a mere 35 miles away. But the Vietnamese had closed off the road to the border and declared it to be a danger zone since there was still fierce fighting between the opposing forces in the area. We were warned that anyone caught in the combat zone would be shot by either the Vietnamese or Angka, no questions asked. This was an obstacle we obviously had not anticipated as we considered our next move. After having made so many sacrifices, and suffering the risks and pain of a dangerous trip, accepting this decision was difficult for us.

As we circulated among the people in the town we heard rumors that the guards stationed at the exit gates of the town could be bribed into turning their heads while allowing people to pass through the barriers. After discussing the pros and cons of our circumstances, we came across five men who told us they could get us to the border if we paid their way. It was clear that we had to make a decision at this time. Going back to Battdambang was not an option, we all agreed. Remaining in our present circumstances was equally undesirable, so we opted for risking the remaining journey to the border. But could we trust these men who were strangers and who might turn us over to Angka to save their own lives?

The answer to that question was straightforward. We would rather risk death, whatever the odds, than continue to live as we had. Late that night, in darkness, we silently approached the guards at the gates. After brief negotiation, the gold they demanded in exchange for their cooperation was agreed upon and they turned their backs as we all slipped outside of the town's borders. When we gathered on the other side we looked back at the town one last time. In our gamble for freedom, had we given up the last vestige of security?

Now we were under the leadership of our five guides. They warned us that we must not talk or make any noise, especially the young children. With that we proceeded through the dense jungle, trying to avoid stepping on anything suspicious or that would produce a sharp noise.

As we made our way, I began to cough while trying desperately to hide the sound. One of the guides told me to hold my small bag of clothing up to my face whenever I felt a need to cough, which made the trip even more difficult for me. After walking a short distance, we were directed to a path that was partially under water. Now we had to proceed through mud which made every step a chore, especially for the men who were carrying the children. My sister-in-law, Savvy, was now finding it extremely difficult to keep up with us and this further endangered our situation. As we continued to slog through the mud, we began to throw off all extra clothing as well as non-essential belongings. After perhaps five or six hours of this tortuous journey, our guides found a spot that was relatively dry where we spent the rest of the night sleeping and resting as best as we could.

The next morning we started out again, walking through thick underbrush and jungle growth. Daylight made the journey a little easier but also increased the risk of being observed by military patrols. By mid-morning, now totally exhausted, we stopped to rest in a cluster of trees which we hoped would conceal our presence. Now, with the hot, dry conditions and our fatigue, thirst was becoming a serious problem. Convinced that there were no patrols in the area and with the hope that we might find a source of water, we decided to go forward. The day was hot and the path difficult. All of us were sick with exhaustion, hunger and thirst; still we knew we had to go on.

Early that evening, we came across an open field that had obviously been the site of a very recent battle. Our guides told us that there had been fighting here less than 48 hours earlier and that this was the most dangerous point of our trip since there were undoubtedly troops still in the area and we would be shot at if we were seen crossing the field. We were told that we must now run across this exposed field to a wooded area about 100 yards ahead. When we were ready, one of the guides gave us the signal and we raced across the open field with whatever strength we could. It was a terrifying experience, since we were now totally exposed and my heart pounded out of fear that at any moment we would hear the sound of gunfire. It seemed like an eternity until I reached the safety of the woods where I simply dropped to the ground, breathing heavily and waiting for the terror in my heart to subside. When I looked back, I realized that Savvy and Chantha were still in the open, struggling desperately to reach the woods. Savvy's husband, Thom, was helping her as best he could and my mother was half-carrying, half-pulling Chantha, now in great pain. I don't know how long we laid there but finally, my heart stopped racing and I was again able to become aware of the world around me. I remember how sweet were the sounds of the birds in the trees above, how fresh the wind felt against my body. Once again, we had defied all the odds and made it safely through another crisis.

As we slowly recovered from the ordeal we smiled and laughed as much for emotional release as for what we had accomplished. We gathered our few possessions and continued our trek to the border, now feeling more confident with the realization that we were only a short distance to our destination. After about two hours we came to a small village occupied by people who spoke Thai. Even though we could not converse with them, they were friendly and helpful. Although we were still in Cambodia, we knew now that our journey to freedom was almost over. For the first time in weeks, I slept well that night feeling comfortable and secure in that small community of strangers.

Early the next morning, when it was still dark and quiet, we prepared ourselves for what we hoped would be the last leg of our escape. Our pace quickened as we approached the border and soon we were running as fast as we could, almost in a state of frenzy. Suddenly, the border was in sight and beyond it a campsite of many people who witnessed our approach with cheers and raised fists. Then finally, exhausted but with tears of laughter we were safe in Thailand, among hundreds of countrymen, women and children who had made a similar journey and were now protected by other Cambodians who were fighting Angka. What a strange and wonderful feeling to feel safer in a foreign land than in our own native country. Slowly, the realization began to grow, we were now beyond the reach of the hated regime. No matter what hardships were in store, we would endure. As long as we were together and free at last from the terror of the last four years.

As we walked through the camp, our clothes ragged and torn, and weary with hunger and thirst, we experienced a sense of ease and freedom among the people that was in stark contrast to life under Angka. Bartering and trade for various goods and necessities was being conducted in the open. We were now a part of this refugee group that had survived the four years of madness that had overtaken our country and we reveled in our rediscovered sense of freedom.

At the center of the camp I noticed a large sign that dominated the area, which I recognized as a Red Cross, however, I did not understand its significance. In that same instant, I noticed a tall, heavy-set man with light brown hair, a mustache and a beard focussing his camera on me. Although I had never seen anyone before who looked so different from me and my people, his demeanor was kind and friendly. With a broad smile he spoke several words to me in a language that I could not understand. I guessed that he might be French or German or American and, although I did not know why he was taking my picture, I thought he might be a journalist reporting to the outside world of the horrors that Cambodia was enduring. If so, perhaps the scenes of my condition and that of my countrymen might help tell the true story to the rest of the world. Perhaps if he, along with the other journalists in the camp shared our experiences with others, then the magnitude of the Angka crimes against humanity would finally be recognized. We would start by referring to the regime by the despised term Khmer Rouge and no longer as Angka. Everyone needed to understand that what happened to Cambodia, a strong, highly cultured, peaceful nation could happen anywhere.

15

True to its reputation, the Red Cross had a well-organized and efficient plan for assisting the hundreds of refugees with their medical and physical needs. Although the camp was dirty and without water, we could endure this hardship given our new-found status. We later discovered that the camp was actually in Cambodia rather than Thailand, but Thai troops along with our own rebel soldiers gave a strong measure of security against Khmer Rouge agents.

We remained at the camp for about two weeks, which gave us some time to review our situation and to plan for our future. In my own case, I thought about the sacrifices my parents had made and that throughout our four-year ordeal, their only concern was for their children with little regard for their own welfare. Even now that we had made our escape and were living in relative security, my father watched our every step, constantly reminding us to maintain a safe distance from the camp's borders. I began to appreciate my parents' love and devotion even more now than at any other time in the past. They never asked for anything for themselves except our love and respect. We were a very lucky family to have survived and I attributed this to the example that they set for us.

During this time, my brother, Thom, who had studied in the

United States in 1974 and could speak some English began to communicate with the American volunteers. He learned from them that Cambodian refugees could move to Thailand and settle there if they chose to do so, but there was no way of knowing how long this might take. Nevertheless, the mere knowledge that this was a possibility produced a feeling of such enthusiasm and hope that we had trouble controlling ourselves.

Now my parents turned their attention to my brother, Thouch and his family, the one missing piece that would make our own family complete. They managed to contact him through letters that were carried to him by refugees returning to Cambodia, pleading with him to join us in the camp prior to our leaving for Thailand. A short while later he actually responded but he told us that he was determined to find his wife's family and that we should continue with our plans. We also sent letters to other family members in an effort to determine their status, trying our best to contact them and to urge them to join us.

Another week passed and my brother, Thom, came to us with the news that we had been approved to go to Thailand. The word was so abrupt and startling, coming after such a short stay in the camp, that I thought he was joking. At first, my parents were in a state of shock, frightened at the prospect of such a major change in their lives, but this reaction quickly turned to happiness because we were together and we knew we would adjust to whatever we encountered. Since we were to leave in less than 24 hours, we frantically prepared for our departure immediately, packing our few belongings and trying to contact family members to inform them of our plans.

By mid-afternoon of the next day, we joined a large group

of refugees already standing next to a number of buses and trucks. Even at this point in time, I was shaking with fear that something would happen at the last moment to upset my dream.

As we approached the buses just before our departure, a group of Cambodians had gathered to the side. Suddenly, they started shouting all sorts of insults at us calling us cowards who were abandoning our country.

I wanted to shout back at them how foolish they were to think that Cambodia could be restored to its former status as a peaceful freedom-loving country. So much had been destroyed including its economy, its family structure, so many lives had been lost, that I knew my beloved country would never be the same. I closed my ears to the insults and instead turned my attention to the buses and the future.

We were led on our bus with the kind assistance of the Red Cross volunteers who did everything they could to make us comfortable. After about a 20-minute wait, the buses and trucks began to move out of the camp, forming a long convoy on the road to freedom. My heart was racing a mile a minute. I was overcome with joy with the realization that this was indeed true and not a dream. As the bus moved out onto the highway and began to pick up speed on the road west to Thailand, I could only say to myself, *"Finally, I am here! I am alive and free."* The air smelled fresh and clean. Even the red dirt blowing up from the road and onto my face had a cleansing effect.

Eventually, I hoped I would be able to put the four years of horror behind me. But for now, the chance to live as a peaceful human being was all I hoped for.

As we drove through the countryside, we saw signs of a normal life that I had forgotten existed. At one point, we passed a school in which children were playing and laughing. I remembered an earlier time when I too could laugh and play, but that seemed a lifetime ago. Still, the sound of their laughter was music to my ears. How fortunate these children were to have been spared the tragedy of my country people, and not to have the best years of their lives taken from them by a cruel, barbaric regime whose only priority was enslavement in body, mind, and spirit.

After about an hour on the road, the bus slowed down as it approached a large tent covered by a roof colored in light blue. As the convoy pulled up to the building and we began to exit the bus, we were approached by a group of Red Cross volunteers who directed us into the main building. I later learned that they were American volunteers, as kind, gentle and caring as possible as if they knew what tragedy we had suffered and that in some small way they might help make up for those experiences.

We were arranged in a queue in front of the tent and administered medication in pill form and in liquid form. We didn't really know what purpose this served, but the demeanor and gentle nature of the volunteers reassured us. We were then separated into groups of 100 and one of the American volunteers directed us to our own quarters. He asked if anyone could speak English and my brother, Thom, volunteered to serve as an interpreter. Again, the sound of this stranger's voice sounded as alien to me as our voices must have sounded to him. I wanted desperately to speak to him and to tell him how grateful we were for his kindness. I thought that perhaps some day I would learn his language and express my gratitude to all of those who were doing their best to help us forget the nightmare. As we began to settle into our new home another American gentleman approached our group and addressed us through a loudspeaker. He asked for three volunteers to help him bring back supplies and my brother, Thom, and two other members of our group walked off with him. They returned within a few minutes carrying large quantities of fruits and vegetables. We were stunned by the sight, having forgotten what it was like to have such a large store of food available for us. We had become so accustomed to constant hunger that we thought this was a natural state. There was complete joy throughout the camp that night as we reveled in our newfound freedom and the simple joy of knowing we needn't worry about where the next meal would come from.

We remained in this camp which we learned was called *Khoa I Dang*, for several months. For the first time since we had been driven from our homes by the Khmer Rouge, a relatively normal routine returned to our lives. During this time, my brother Thom's wife, Savvy, with the aid of the Red Cross, gave birth to their first child, a fine baby boy who was a source of great joy to all of us. If there was any doubt that we had made the right decision by leaving Cambodia it was dispelled by this new addition to our family. Shortly thereafter, our happiness was complete when my brother, Thouch, and his wife, Navy, made their way to our camp. We all rejoiced at their arrival although we were saddened to hear that they were unable to locate two of Navy's seven siblings. However, they learned that the other five survived the terrible ordeal.

There were many other refugees who continued to pour into the camp every day. Fortunately, aid and assistance from all over the world also continued to arrive. It was wonderful to know that people from everywhere were becoming aware of the tragedy in Cambodia and were contributing to our recovery. I remember seeing signs from different agencies, U.N.H.C.R. and G.V.A. and others in languages I couldn't understand, all of whom played their part in this vast effort.

Almost from the first day in camp, I was fascinated by the many foreigners who had invested time and effort at obviously great personal sacrifice to come to the assistance of strangers in a distant part of the world. In particular, as I learned to recognize the differences between our rescuers, I was intrigued by the American volunteers who were so open and friendly that I couldn't help but want to learn more about their country. So when we were given an opportunity to continue our education and to learn English, I jumped at the chance. As with all of the others, our English teacher was kind and patient. At first, the language seemed difficult and awkward. Moreover, I was too shy to practice it out of fear of being ridiculed and laughed at. Within several weeks, however, and through the encouragement of the teacher and the other pupils, I was able to say a few simple phrases and was able to write the alphabet. One of the first books we were given was the Bible which was written in Cambodian, and this introduced me to the fascinating religion of the West. Now, the stories that my brother, Thom, told me of his experiences in America began to exert a powerful appeal. Slowly, the rest of my dream began to emerge. It involved living in a country where people were free of oppression and where opportunities to learn and grow were open to everyone. Where famine and ragged clothes were no longer commonplace. In my mind, I equated my dream with America, and nothing anyone said would shake me from my belief.

16

We had been living in Khoa I Dang for over six months. During this time Than married *Youen.* While we celebrated this event as a part of our new lives, many others despaired of the circumstances, some of whom even returned to Cambodia, despite the continuing warfare there. I never lost sight of my dream. Finally, one day we received word that our family had been selected for possible emigration to another country. The procedure was a long and complicated one and while we knew that some day we might be considered for this, we were still faced with many uncertainties. First of all, if we were approved we didn't know what our destination might be. Some of the refugee families were sent to France, some to England, others to Germany, and still others to the United States. Then, there were interviews to be conducted, tests to be taken, papers to be completed and questions to be answered. Above all, sponsors had to be found who were willing to underwrite our entire rehabilitation. As our time to leave became a reality my parents were faced with a cruel dilemma. They had sacrificed everything and taken incredible risks, just so their children could leave the harsh life of what Cambodia had become, for the safety and security of another country, and they were elated now that this was a virtual certainty. On the other hand, they would be leaving their mothers and other relatives and friends behind. The decision created much anguish for all of us. In the end, however, we knew that remaining in the camp or even returning to Cambodia would not improve the lives of any of us. Sadly, we recognized that the Cambodia we loved would never return and that leaving was the only way.

As the time grew nearer to our departure and we were given reason to believe that an American sponsor had been found, I could scarcely breathe or conceal my excitement. On the day my father and Thom returned from the central quarters I ran to greet them and I could tell from the huge grins on their faces: It was time. My dream had turned to reality. We were going to America. I cried and laughed at the same time. My sister, Chan, and I hugged one another and then the whole family joined in. My mother broke away from us and gave thanks that our whole family had survived the nightmare of the Khmer Rouge. It was a moment of such an emotional pitch that it will live with me forever.

Now we were making our final preparations to leave. My brother, Thouch, and his family were unable to accompany us, but we were reassured that their passage would also be arranged in time. On the day we were to leave, we said our goodbyes and boarded a bus which was to take us to *Chun Bori*, the final repatriation camp about two hours drive from Khoa I Dang.

When we arrived there that afternoon, we learned that we would be subjected to another interview process which might delay or even change our plans. My heart sank at this news. To have gone through so much, and to be so close, only to discover that the outcome was still in doubt, left me in despair.

We spent five days waiting for the interview during which time I went through the tortures of the damned. Finally, we were all called to the main camp where we were arranged before a desk with a yellow file on top. Within moments, the interviewer entered the office along with a Cambodian interpreter and the questions proceeded: how many children in the family, had any died, what were our ages, any family history of disease, and so on. Each of us was interviewed and with each response, the interviewer turned to his file to verify our answers with his source of information. Since it was not our custom to establish exact birth dates, my sister, Chan and I, had picked our "days" the night before. But this slight deception made me extremely anxious and I almost trembled at the thought that my response would give me away and we would be denied our exit from Cambodia. At the end of the interview, our interrogator indicated through the interpreter that our papers were in order, but that we would have to go through additional interviews before the final decision was made.

Now, all we could do was wait for the next step in the process. We busied ourselves as best as we could, trying not to think about the possibility that we still could be denied permission to leave for America.

Exactly two weeks later, our names were on the list of families scheduled for the next interview at 1:00. We walked over to the camp headquarters together in silence, each of us wondering and hoping that this would be the last obstacle in our plans for the future. As we waited to be called, I felt the tension mount in me once again out of fear that I might say something that would hurt our chances. Finally, our names were called and we were directed into the same office where we had been interviewed two weeks earlier. Similar thoughts raced through my mind as we stood and waited before our new interrogator. He was tall with red hair and a full red beard and as he looked through our file, I could tell he was displeased about the information before him. Finally, he told us through the interpreter that our application could not be approved because there were married members who had to be considered as separate family units. Consequently, we would have to be interviewed again, at a later date, this time as independent families. This included my oldest brother, Choeun, and his wife, Kim Run, my fourth oldest brother, Than, and his wife, Youen, and my sister, Chantha, even though her husband had died.

We were confused and disappointed by this decision, but once again I was determined not to let this experience spoil my dream, and I tried to maintain a busy schedule.

Finally, after about three weeks, we were called for the next interview, only to find that the same man with the red hair and beard was to be our interrogator once again. My heart sank when we were ushered into his office, but he was much more pleasant this time. Nevertheless, the questions he asked were more personal and difficult to answer on this occasion. In particular, when he asked my mother about her mother's circumstances, my mother broke down and cried, barely able to respond through her emotions. She finally answered by saying that we had been unable to account for her whereabouts as well as those of other family members. Having to review all of these events was a heartbreaking experience for all of us. But we had answered honestly and with conviction, and we left not knowing what our status was. Two days later, however, we heard that our interview had been well received and that we had been approved to continue to the next step.

Less than a week later, we learned that my oldest brother, Choeun, and his family had completed their interviews and had been approved to leave for America. This was the best news we had received in five years, and we were overjoyed that they were now going to start a new life free of the nightmare still going on in Cambodia.

The next day we helped his family board the bus that would take them to the airport and ultimate freedom in a place called Virginia, a beautiful sounding name. As we said our goodbyes, we vowed that we would all once again be reunited in our new country.

Exactly one week later, our final interview was scheduled. This turned out to be more of a formality than anything else, and now the only remaining barrier was the chest x-ray to check for communicable diseases. We waited another two weeks, which seemed an eternity, but finally the results came back that we were free of disease and that we had passed all the requirements. Our application was approved—we could go to America! It was a strange experience. In my dreams I always imagined receiving the good news by hugging my loved ones and crying; demonstrating our happiness without restraint. When the final word came, however, I was almost numb with joy. We were all smiling and my mother was crying, but the importance of that event was almost too much to comprehend or truly appreciate. There was no way to understand why our lives had been spared in the face of the devastation we had witnessed. And now to leave it all behind and to start over again in the land of freedom and opportunity was more than anyone could have thought possible at the height of our despair.

17

The next several days were full of happiness as we planned our future and strived to learn as much about our new country as possible.

Two weeks after my brother and his family left we received a letter from him describing, in the most wonderful terms, their experience in America. His sponsors were extremely kind, helping them to adjust to their new lives in Virginia. I read his letter over and over. His description sounded like they were in a make-believe land, a land that yielded kindness and good fortune rather than pain and hatred. It seemed even better than I had imagined. The day we waited for finally arrived. Our names appeared on the list of families approved for departure on October 22, 1980, only four days away now. The news left me literally shaking with happiness. My dream was about to become reality.

The next four days offered many new and exciting experiences. We were given a book entitled "You're on Your Way" which was printed in Cambodian and Vietnamese, explaining a world of details related to our forthcoming trip. It described the airplane trip, what food Americans ate, how they dressed, and so forth. We learned what our responsibilities as American citizens would be as well as the benefits and privileges, all of which were overwhelming coming from a background of terror and oppression.

The day before we were to leave, my mother made the one last sacrifice still available to her. She insisted that we should not enter into our new lives dressed in torn and dirty clothing. That morning she sold grandmother's wedding ring, the one remaining piece of jewelry that she had refused to part with, even during periods of starvation, and bought each of us a new outfit. I would rather she had kept the ring than given me my first pair of blue jeans, but her love for us was so great that she never thought twice about the decision.

The night before we were scheduled to leave, I hardly slept at all, given my state of excitement. When morning came, I was well ahead of everyone in preparing for our departure. Now we were on our way to board the bus that would take us to the airport in Bangkok. There were about 200 people in addition to my family. As we made our way on what was to be our last contact with the refugee camp, many of our country people were gathered around my family group and wishing us well. Some of the crowd gently touched us as if in this small gesture we would be taking a part of them to the new country.

My brother, Than, and his family and my sister, Chantha, accompanied us to the bus, embracing us for what we hoped would only be a short time before they would join us in America, and our family would be together again.

We took our seats and the bus drove off leaving the hopeful behind. Perhaps they too would soon be making this same trip. Very shortly, we approached the beautiful city of Bangkok, ancient and revered capital of Thailand, famous for its religious temples and as a cultural and trading center. It was wonderful to see a big city again, the streets and houses clean and well-kept, markets busy with people buying and selling all sorts of merchandise and the magnificent temples, symbols of religious tradition thousands of years old. They reminded me of the temples of Cambodia, now almost completely destroyed by the Khmer Rouge in their frenzy to erase all of our own traditions.

Our bus came to a stop at a large building outside the airport. As we exited, we were given instructions to form a line and wait for our names to be called. Suddenly, the skies opened and a torrent of rain burst down upon us while we waited, now wet and cold, to be asked inside. Within a few minutes, an American official appeared and started to read names from a list that he held. Our names were called and we were led into a small building which was crowded with scores of other refugees, all of us gathered here for the final step, the plane that would arrive to take us to America. We moved to a far area of the room which served as a place to sleep that night, since we were informed that our flight was scheduled for the following day. Although we spent the night on a cement floor in a crowded room with dozens of others no one complained, and this certainly didn't dampen my enthusiasm.

Early the next morning we heard an announcement over a loudspeaker requesting each family to send one person to the office for final instructions. My brother, Thom, left immediately while we waited anxiously for his return. After a short while we saw him smiling as he made his way back through the crowd. He told us that we would be going to a place called Oklahoma, a beautiful but hard to pronounce name. So now, the final question had been answered and after another brief wait our name was called to prepare for the bus ride to the airport. Although it was now late at night, and we had been going at a high pitch for several days, we were too excited to rest and relax now. We boarded the bus and drove the short distance to the airport. We drove through the gates into the airport itself and the sight was overwhelming to someone like me who had never seen anything as immense and exciting as this. It was now about 2:30 in the morning, but you would never know it from the high state of activity around us. We stepped off the bus and were shown to a waiting area. After about two hours, the ground under us started shaking as if an earthquake had started. This was a confusing and frightening experience until we were told that our plane had arrived and our mood quickly changed.

We were then formed into a line and passed through the security guards at the gate. Since most of us had few or no possessions, we completed this part of the routine very quickly and then we were moving up the ramp on to the plane. As I boarded the plane I was trembling with such excitement, I thought my heart would explode. Perhaps the full realization of what we had achieved caused the emotional state. My God, I thought, we had indeed made it. My whole family and I had survived the worst evils of Pol Pot and his killers. We had lived through death, starvation, beatings, and executions, every conceivable practice of inhumanity, and we were now on our way to live in peace. As I reached the top of the stairs leading into the cabin of the airplane, I paused for one brief moment to look back and pictured in my mind the land of Cambodia that I would never see again. A place that I had once loved and called home. I said goodbye to my country and all of the memories both good and bad. Goodbye Cambodia. I once loved you, and now I must place my affection on a new land on the other side of the world, far from everything that was familiar.

We entered the airplane and walked into a totally new world of lights and buttons and air conditioning. The seats were clean and comfortable, there were windows to look out and a general atmosphere of relaxation and ease. If this was a sample of what America was like, then the real thing must be paradise.

I helped my mother in her seat and turned to look into the face of the most beautiful woman in the world. She was tall and thin with long golden hair and perfect skin. She was smiling down at us and helped us get comfortable. Throughout our entire trip, she came by numerous times, making sure our questions were answered and our needs were met. I will never forget that woman and her kindness to my family.

We sat back in our seats, a million questions racing through our minds. Suddenly, the airplane began to move away from the terminal and taxied to the take-off point. The engines began to roar and we started down the runway, racing faster and faster, the scene outside becoming a blur. I looked out the window to say goodbye to my country one last time. Perhaps, some day, I would return to Cambodia, but only if the violence was gone. The wheels of the plane left the ground and with that sensation, a feeling that our agony was really over.

18

The long trip on the plane was an introduction to a new way of life. The food that was offered to us seemed so alien to our taste that we existed on water and fruit alone during our flight over the Pacific. After many hours of flying we prepared to land at a big city which we were told was called San Francisco. As I looked down at the approaching land, a scene of utter amazement spread out before me. So many boats, cars, tall buildings—I had never visualized a community of such magnitude and complexity, yet also clean and peaceful looking. How fortunate the citizens of this city were to be living in such a paradise. When we finally landed, we were taken directly to the other side of the terminal where we boarded another airplane which would take us to our final destination—Oklahoma. As we waited for our departure, and night time approached, I had more time to look about and to appreciate the scene before me. The buildings, although off in the distance, still seemed enormous, and now the many lights turned the darkness into light. But what impressed me the most was the people walked about in an atmosphere of freedom. They were well-dressed, relaxed, without restraint. How different this all was from Cambodia.

Within a short time we were airborne once again. Our translators informed us that we would arrive in Oklahoma at

11:00 p.m. where we would be met by our sponsors. We were also told that the weather there was quite cold and each of us was issued a heavy warm coat and a pair of thick socks. This aroused a great deal of curiosity and humor since we had never seen such clothing before.

Now our airplane started its descent and our excitement increased as our destination, Oklahoma City, began to take shape before our eyes. Once again, I experienced a sense of wonderment as the magnitude of the community became clear. Again, hundreds of tall buildings, thousands of lights stretching as far as the eye could see, cars beyond calculation speeding in every direction on a vast network of roads. America was truly a land of great wealth and, even more importantly, stability. As we realized our dream was coming true, an incredible feeling of joy came over us.

The plane landed and taxied to the terminal. We walked off the plane and approached a large group of people who had been waiting for our arrival. A man stepped forward and asked us our names. He introduced himself as a Laotian who was to be our sponsor. Then he brought us over to meet his beautiful wife and children and welcomed us to the United States of America. In the midst of this scene of family love and the realization that our ordeal was at an end, we started to cry from the depths of our souls. He understood our reactions completely and gently assisted us to his car. Everywhere we looked we saw friendly, smiling faces. The airport itself was a paradise of beautiful architecture, greenery and hospitality. We were driven to an apartment in Oklahoma City and given $200.00 each that would meet our immediate expenses until we had found employment and to prepare us for taking care of our own needs. He indicated that he would assist us as much as possible and that as we became independent he would turn his attention to other refugees. He was true to his word and we shall always be grateful to this wonderful man and his wife who made it possible for us to make the transition from Cambodian refugees to American citizens.

19

The days passed into months and we gradually adjusted to our new country. Each of us knew that to improve our circumstances we would have to secure jobs. All of us found employment in short order and accumulated enough assets to purchase a home. Finally we had, once again, after so long, our very own home.

In the early summer of 1983 I was working as a cashier in an Oklahoma City restaurant when I met an American man who showed me great kindness and understanding. Over a period of several weeks I began to realize that this gentle man was special to me. He assisted me in learning English and in understanding many American customs which were puzzling me. He continued to help me and wanted to know more of my own circumstances and at times even seemed impressed with me. Within a very short time I trusted this man and wanted him to meet my parents. He agreed to this and arrived at our modest home to meet everyone in my family. At first my mother was rather suspicious of this American man named Bill who showed so much interest in her youngest child. Within time, however, my mother and father realized that Bill would soon become their son-in-law.

In August of that same year, Bill and I were married, a little more than three years after my escape. I was now *Sophal Leng Stagg*. It was at this time that I adopted my new first name, *Sophie*, which to me sounded very much like my real name, as well as a nice American name.

We lived outside Oklahoma City for the next few years enjoying a life that I had dreamed about just a few short years earlier.

On June 23, 1986, at the age of 20, another part of my dream became a reality with the birth of a healthy ten pound son. Our baby was brought into this world as *William Chester Stagg*, a beautiful child who brought tears of joy to my eyes. I held my son close to me, promising him that he would have a wonderful life far away from the evil that I once knew.

During my pregnancy I was tutored by my husband and continued to study English to prepare myself for another very important upcoming event. I was determined to become an American citizen as soon as I was able. Four months after the birth of my son I took the Oath of Citizenship at the Federal Building in Oklahoma City. I was now an American.

Three wonderful years passed with all of the happiness any person could expect. My husband and I and our son moved to Florida and were anxiously awaiting the arrival of our second child.

In the Spring of 1991, on Memorial Day, our second son was born. He was a beautiful boy who added great happiness to an already wonderful family. We named him *Michael Jacob*, a special name for a special child. We brought him home and immediately shared him with his big brother Billy and to this day, the pair are inseparable.

Once again our family rejoiced at the recent events and continued to thrive. Finally, in the summer of 1994, Bill and I became the proud parents of identical twin boys, an event that only underscored all of the miraculous experiences involved in our escape, since multiple births are so rare among Asian women. I can honestly say that everything I had hoped for had come to pass, and my dream had become reality. Our sons were named *Tyler James* and *Trevor John*, a lovely finale to the family.

At this point my life has changed in the most extraordinary manner imaginable. I can truly enjoy the life of a full-fledged American citizen with a wonderful husband, beautiful children and the knowledge that we are safe to experience the greatness of this generous country.

Yet, I often think of those who were left behind and who still suffer and struggle for mere survival. My husband and I continue to help the people of Southeast Asia as co-founders of the *Southeast Asian Mercy Fund*. I know there are others there with dreams, just like I had as a young Cambodian girl. I am determined to help make those dreams come true.

When they are older, I will tell my sons of the sacrifices we endured from 1975 to 1980, and of their continuing responsibility to help in the struggle for freedom for people all over the world. We must never forget what happened in Cambodia, and is still happening today.

Twenty years ago, a regime intent on mass annihilation gained control of my former country, causing one of the most unimaginable horrors the world has ever known. My children, and all the children of the world must know that we have been placed at risk and that evils must be confronted. I believe that this fact must be taught to the children of the world, all children, regardless of race or color. They need to know the power and strength of love to combat the influence of tyrants.

The struggle to eliminate oppression in the world continues.

Epilog

Of the millions of families that fell victim to the Khmer Rouge, the Lengs may have been one of the very few that survived relatively intact throughout the ordeal. Although there is no completely adequate explanation as to why some families endure such experiences and others do not, mere circumstance may, of course, determine these outcomes. Simply being in the wrong place at the wrong time often makes the difference between living and dying. Beyond these chance factors, however, the bonds of support and willingness to sacrifice for one another may also enter into the equation. If there is any truth to this theory, the Leng family is living testimony to it.

As of March 1998, Sophie's parents Kim and Na were alive and well, living a new life in the Dallas area. Both parents, now in their seventies, enjoy busy days, surrounded by the love and devotion of their family. This wonderful couple watch with pride as their loved ones, for whom they made countless sacrifices, continue to grow and prosper.

Sophie's oldest brother Choeun and his wife Kim Run continue to reside in Oklahoma city and have three beautiful children. Their two daughters, Kara and Karin, both of whom were within days of dying from starvation, are presently enrolled in college in Oklahoma. Karin, who was literally nursed back to health by Sophie's mother, has earned a scholarship to medical school. Kara graduated with honors and is now married and living in Dallas. Their younger brother Woothy is in high school in Oklahoma City.

The Leng's second oldest child, Thom and his wife Savvy, also live in the Dallas area with their two children. Their son Rithy, with whom Savvy was pregnant when the family crossed the border into Thailand, is now a high school student and Kim and Na's oldest grandson. Their second child, a beautiful girl named Amy, was born in America.

Sophie's brother Thouch and his wife Navy have also remained in the Oklahoma area, and their two daughters, Siala and Stephanie, are excellent students in the school system there.

Chantha, Sophie's oldest sister lives in the Dallas area with her son Danith. She has devoted her life to him and her family and friends, always doing for others and never asking for anything in return.

Sophie's brother Than and his wife Youen also live in the Oklahoma City area and are hard-working parents of a son, Robert, and a daughter, Monica.

Thoeun, the youngest male of the Leng family, married a

Cambodian girl, Ny, and moved to the Dallas area to be close to Kim and Na. They have a son, Michael Steven.

Sophie's next oldest sister Chan, who took Sophie's place in the killing fields, is now living in the Dallas area with her husband Sovan, a Cambodian refugee who lost his parents and six siblings to the Khmer Rouge. They have two children, Jason and Jessica.

As is true of all those who remember what life was like before the Cambodian government was overthrown, the Lengs mourn the loss of those whose lives were sacrificed during the Khmer rouge holocaust:

Thoeun's wife Ny: Father executed

Chan's husband Sovan: Both parents executed, six siblings died in the death camps.

Thouch's wife Navy: Both parents died in death camps.

Thom's wife Savvy: Brother Haing beaten to death as witnessed by Na Leng; sister Sony died eating poisonous fruit.

Than's wife Youen: Both parents and all her siblings died in the death camps.

Sophie's mother Na: Younger sister Kong, her husband and their seven children; younger brother, his wife and their three children, all executed.

Sophie's father Kim: Brother's two sons and entire families
                        executed.

Choeun's wife Kim Run:Younger sister, her husband and their
                      two children, executed.

In 1992, Kim Run returned to Cambodia to search for her sister Huoy and her family. It was on that trip that she learned that they had all been executed by the Khmer rouge during the purge of all intellectuals, simply because Huoy's husband was a college professor. Their graves have never been found.

*Sophal with
Tyler James
1994*

*Kim Leng
with
grandsons
Tyler and
Trevor
1994*

*Na Leng with
grandchildren
Tyler, Trevor,
Billy and
Michael
1995*